Ready-to-Use Social Studies Activities for the Elementary Classroom

Debra Seabury
Susan Peeples

The Center for Applied Research in Education
West Nyack, New York

Library of Congress Cataloging-in-Publication Data

Seabury, Debra.
    Ready-to-use social studies activities for the elementary
classroom / Debra Seabury, Susan Peeples.
        p.   cm.
    ISBN 0-87628-788-7
    1. Social sciences–Study and Teaching (Elementary)—United
States.   2. Education, Elementary—United States—Activity programs.
3. Interdisciplinary approach in education—United States.
I. Peeples, Susan.   II. Title.
LB1584.S42   1989
372.83'0973—dc20   89-39113
                                                                          CIP

ISBN 0-87628-788-7

10 9 8 7 6 5 4 3

Printed in the United States of America

About the Authors

DEBRA SEABURY earned her B.A. degree from Western Washington University, where she majored in elementary education with an English minor. She has taught grades 4 through 6.

SUSAN PEEPLES also received her B.A. degree from Western Washington University, majoring in elementary education with minors in art and library science. She has taught grades 1 through 6 as well as served as a remedial specialist in both reading and math.

With 25 years' combined experience in the elementary classroom, the authors are currently teaching in the Ferndale (Washington) Public Schools, where both have done work on the development of goals and curriculum. They have been writing together for five years and are also coauthors of *Ready-to-Use Science Activities for the Elementary Classroom*, published by The Center for Applied Research in Education in 1987. Several of their articles have appeared in *Oasis* magazine, and both are contributing authors to The Center's *Primary Teacher's Ready-to-Use Activities Program*.

CONTENTS

Contents

Contents

About This Resource

Ready-to-Use Social Studies Activities for the Elementary Classroom offers classroom teachers practical materials for teaching social studies content while reinforcing basic skills. Designed to stimulate interest, these interdisciplinary activities give elementary students practice in reading, math, and writing skills while helping them expand their understanding of history and geography.

Developed by two teachers with over 25 years' combined teaching experience, these activities are clearly written and easy to use. Each is complete, reproducible, and ready for immediate use by students for discovery and review.

Ready-to-Use Social Studies Activities for the Elementary Classroom is organized for your convenience into five sections:

- "Section One: For the Teacher" includes social studies bulletin board suggestions, project ideas for art and creative writing, and full-page forms, calendars, and social studies certificates of merit.

- "Section Two: Native Americans" is divided into four units—Woodland Indians, Plains Indians, Southwest Indians, and Coastal Indians. Each unit offers reproducible activity sheets for your students covering topics such as "Sacajawea," "Picture Writing," "A Parfleche," "Kachinas," and "Sandpainting."

- "Section Three: American Heritage" examines the "Exploration of the New World," "Settlement," "Becoming a Nation," and "Government." The activities in this section introduce your students to such topics as "The Aztecs," "The Lost Colony," "Linsey-Woolsey," "Your Representatives," and "U.S. Coins" through a variety of formats including word searches and crossword puzzles.

- "Section Four: World Regions" explores the three major regions of the world—"The Tropics," "The Temperate Zone," and "The Arctic." Your students will enjoy such activities as "How Cold Is It?", "Atolls," "The Saraha," and "Animals of the Temperate Regions."

- "Section Five: Answer Key" provides complete answers for the activity sheets in Sections Two, Three, and Four.

These materials offer you great flexibility in selecting activities for a six-week study of our heritage, for example, or a three-week government unit, or a one-week concentration on elections. Because all of the activities are laid out for you step-by-step, you can quickly plan and prepare your lessons, saving yourself valuable time for quality instruction.

Through the variety of suggested activities and experiences in *Ready-to-Use Social Studies Activities for the Elementary Classroom*, you can lead your students through a wide range of concepts and discoveries. Students will grow in their understanding of history, geography, and themselves.

Debra Seabury
Susan Peeples

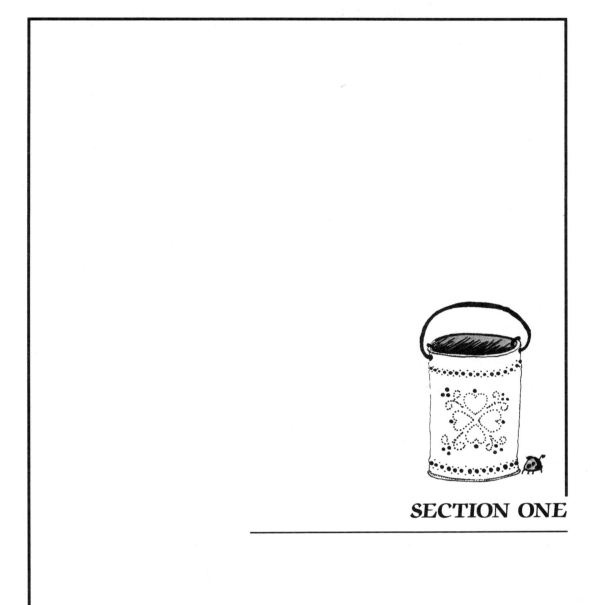

SECTION ONE

FOR THE TEACHER

Take a moment to look at this book and to get a feel for its content and structure. *Ready-to-Use Social Studies Activities for the Elementary Classroom* is divided into five sections.

- Section One is directed to the teacher and includes teacher aides and teacher-directed activities.

- Sections Two, Three, and Four are directed to the student and contain student activity pages.

- Section Five offers a complete answer key to the activity pages. Let's take a closer look at each part of this book.

TEACHER AIDS

The teacher aids begin with two forms. The resources form is an organizational tool enabling you to keep a current list of "extras." Each time you teach your units, you have only to add new resources. These listings eliminate searching for names, numbers, and titles each time you use your units. In compiling your lists, be sure to check public libraries as well as your school's resource center. Government agencies and professional organizations are also good sources.

The calendar page is for planning and scheduling your units. Reproduce as many pages as necessary. After looking over the material and your completed resources list, select the lessons, activities, and resources that best meet your objectives. Begin filling in your calendar. Don't forget to schedule films and guests well in advance.

Bulletin boards are excellent teaching tools, and those suggested here reinforce the content of these social studies activities. They can be easily copied by using an opaque or overhead projector. Of course, you can adapt the ideas to your available space and materials.

TEACHER-DIRECTED ACTIVITIES

The teacher-directed activities and art projects are integral to each section of this book. These concrete activities reinforce the content of each unit while leading to new discoveries. Art lessons and activities get students actively involved with learning, so use as many as your scheduling allows.

The themes of this book are expanded through creative writing. These lessons explore beyond the basic social studies content and stretch the students' imagination and creativity. Each creative writing activity is complete with reproducible pages for the presentation of the students' final work.

All too often, units have a way of "fizzling out." Culminations and student awards keep interest high right up to the last days of your social studies units. Everyone is left with positive feelings of accomplishment.

GETTING STUDENTS STARTED

The student part of Ready-to-Use Social Studies Activities has three sections: Native Americans, Heritage, and Geography. Each section includes similar types of materials that are discussed in detail below.

Vocabulary

Three types of activities to introduce and expand vocabulary are used in this book.

- Word searches expose students to new vocabulary specific to the social studies content.
- Crossword puzzles develop and reinforce vocabulary.
- Handwriting pages provide handwriting practice but also reinforce vocabulary and develop spelling skills. These handwriting pages can also be used for recording definitions or writing sentences.

Reading

This book uses three reading formats. The modified cloze activities give students information and practice in context word analysis. The student chooses the best word from the listed choices. Comprehension pages with accompanying illustrations also cover basic social studies content. They address a variety of learning styles by challenging children to understand visually displayed information.

The "ready, set, go" selections are readings about interesting or unusual topics related to the specific unit topics. Each of these "ready, set, go" pages has a prereading activity, the reading itself, and comprehension checks. Whenever possible, expand the interest these selections create by displaying related items or additional reading material.

Math

The math lessons included in this book are based on the content of each unit. These lessons emphasize basic operations. They are not designed to introduce new math skills, but rather encourage students to exercise logic and reason in problem solving.

Puzzles

A variety of puzzle formats give students opportunities to encounter information in new and interesting ways. Use these puzzles with your whole class, small groups, or with individual students. Puzzles also work well in activity centers or as homework assignments to be shared with parents.

Quick Checks

Ready-to-Use Social Studies Activities uses quick checks for review and evaluation. Each of the three sections concludes with a one-page review of the material specific to that section. These quick checks may be used to evaluate student progress or for a review practice.

Resources

Audio-Visuals (films, filmstrips, etc.)

number   *title*

_____   _____

_____   _____

_____   _____

_____   _____

_____   _____

_____   _____

Books (magazines, prints, transparencies, etc.)

title   *author/publisher*

_____   _____

_____   _____

_____   _____

_____   _____

_____   _____

_____   _____

Speakers-Field Trips-Others

Planning Calendar

MONDAY	TUESDAY	WEDNESDAY	THURSDAY	FRIDAY

Social Studies Bulletin Boards

Enlarge the United States map with an opaque or overhead projector. Divide map into regions. Have students color the symbols for each region. Attach traditionally dressed paper doll figures to the board. Make pockets to hold cards. Develop the sets of cards as each region is being studied. At the end of each lesson, students decide the words to be written on cards. Cards might include names of tribes found in each region, types of homes, methods of transportation, art forms, common food sources, and cut outs of pictures or drawings.

This bulletin board can also be used as a question and answer game. Begin by dividing the class into four groups. Each group writes twenty question cards with the correct answers on the back for their region. Put the cards in the region pocket holders. Students can play as partners or teams to see who can correctly answer the most questions.

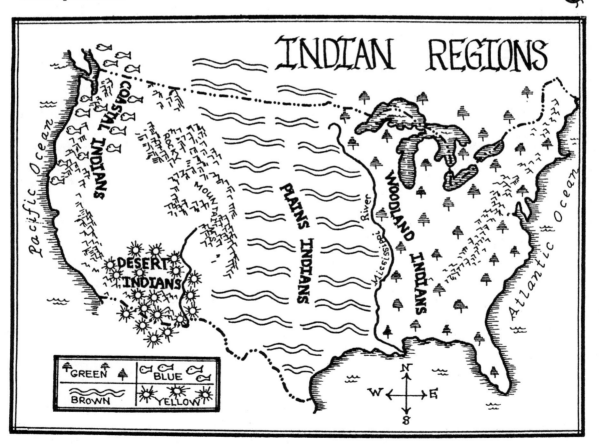

Students will be actively involved in the "Footsteps in Time" bulletin board. Use green background. Attach yellow path. Add title. Cut soles and heels for footprints from black paper. You will need *one* print for every *two* students. Use white pencil, ink or chalk to write events on the soles. Write matching dates on the heels. Choose some unusual events and dates as well as those you are currently studying.

To assemble the trail, give each student one half of a print (either a sole or a heel). Direct students to find the person with the matching piece. After students are paired, have the order themselves chronologically. Attach matched footprints to path.

Extend the activity by having students make prints for other events. Disassemble, reorder, and reassemble. If space is limited, run the prints off the board onto the wall. You may want to switch two dates each day and have students search for the errors.

"The Whole Wide World" lets students place features in their proper locations on a map of the world. Use blue background for the water. Cut land areas of green. String or narrow ribbon marks the tropics, equator, and prime meridian. Use premade cards for the continents and oceans.

Supply stars, blank labels and pens for adding students' own discoveries. Pins with colored heads are good for marking cities. A small piece of masking tape makes a flag for labeling.

Disassemble and reassemble often. Expand the use of your display. Consider adding countries, cities, products, time zones, landforms, etc. You may want to make a key booklet available for students to self-check. Hang by a string to one side of the map.

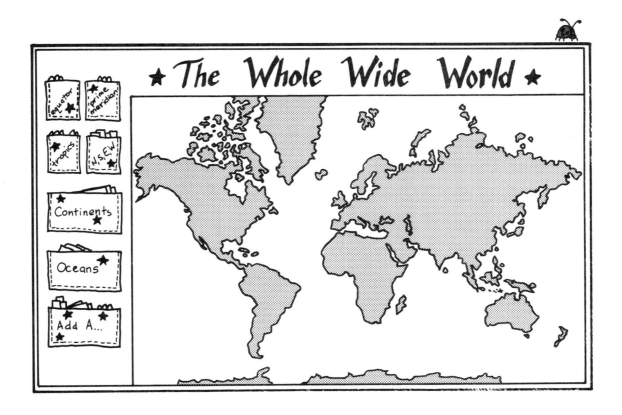

Social Studies Art Projects

Clay Pots

Pottery was a craft of Native Americans that your students can experience. Two types of simple pots can be constructed by most elementary students. For either type you will need a ball of clay about 3″ in diameter for each student. If you do not have access to a kiln, use clay that will harden as it air dries. Some clay is available that can be baked in a conventional oven.

Pinch pots are the simplest. Start with a ball of clay. Stick your thumb into the middle of the ball. Using thumb and fingers, pinch the clay to form the walls of your pot. Use your thumb to press and shape the bottom.

For coil pots first form clay into long ropes. Carefully coil the rope around itself to form the bottom of the pot. Then wind the ropes around, building on top of the bottom's edge. Continue coiling upwards to finish the walls. As you wind the coils, wet edges as each new layer is applied to help them stick together. Smooth the pot inside and out.

Decorate your pots with Native American designs. Use your pot to store treasured items or as a gift for a special friend.

Sandpainting

Your students can simulate sandpainting in your classroom. You will need at least three different colors of sand. Black, yellow, and red are good choices. You will also need white glue thinned with equal amounts of water, paint brushes, oak tag, and clear acrylic spray.

On the background of tagboard, have students draw a simple outline picture. You may suggest Native American subjects. For younger students you may want to make copies of simple designs for them to choose.

Decide on the colors to be used in each area of your picture. Start with the darkest color. Brush glue *thinly* on areas for one color only. Sprinkle with sand. Tip and shake or tap gently to remove excess sand. Let dry before adding another color. This may take overnight. Repeat with other colors to complete your design. Spray finished pictures with acrylic.

Scenes From the Past

Students can experience scenes from the past on a small scale by constructing dioramas. Boxes should be about 12″ x 12″ x 18″. Canned goods often come in this size box. Check grocery stores. Your other supplies will depend of your subject Paint, paper, cardstock, markers, fabric scraps, and glue are basic.

Choose subjects with plenty of detail. Some good choices are a Native American village, a colonial home, or early settlement. Students need to research subjects to make their dioramas authentic.

The simplest figures are drawn on cardstock and cut out. Make them stand up by making flaps at the bottom to glue to the floor. You can also leave figures free-standing so they can be moved about the scene. More elaborate scale models may be constructed of matchboxes, small stick, clay, pipestems, etc. Encourage imagination and display with pride.

Speak Out!

By making posters, students become aware of their voice in a democracy. Students should first choose and research their topic. Students might select a national, state, or local subject. Some good choices are anti-smoking/drugs themes, local park or pool bond issues, or state litter campaigns.

You will need poster paper, paints, and/or markers. Discuss poster design. Explain that a poster is really selling an idea or point of view. Stress a brief, powerful message, and bold design. You may want to supply large stencils or letter patterns.

Display posters where others will see them and receive their messages. Place them around your school or community. Check with local businesses. One or more may be delighted to display your students' work.

Soap Carving

Every culture of the world does some form of carving. Soap is a material that can be "whittled" easily to make simple animal figures. Have each child select an animal to carve. Choose creatures that have rounded, bulky shapes. Try to avoid creatures with thin body parts that would break off easily. Each child will need a bar of soap and a table knife or paring knife. Encourage children to turn the soap as they carve to create a piece that looks good when viewed from any angle. Keep the bottom surface flat so that the animal will stand.

Patchwork Quilts

Patchwork quilts were a traditional craft of the colonists and pioneers. Fabric scraps were sewn together to make beautiful designs. Patchwork blocks are made of rectangles, squares, triangles, hexagons, diamonds, and arcs. These shapes are arranged on a grid of squares – with 4, 9, 16, 25, and sometimes 36 squares to a block. The patterns are recognized by their number of blocks; a 4-patch block, 9-patch block etc. Hand out sheets of 1 inch grid paper to students. Show them examples of traditional patchwork patterns. Then have them create patterns of their own using 4, 9, 16, or 25 squares and geometric designs. Encourage students to add patterns to their designs by including dots, stripes, flowers, etc., and by using bright colors to complete their patchwork block.

4 patch block

9 patch block

16 patch block

25 patch block

Social Studies Creative Writing

Letters to Representatives

Stress the importance of individual participation in a democracy by having students write letters to their elected representatives. They may write to local, state, or national officials. Names and addresses of government officials are available from your public library.

Choose issues of real concern to your students. Encourage student to select a topic they feel strongly about and write from their personal point of view. Discuss correct business letter form. Brief, specific letters are best. Proofread rough drafts and correct errors. Transfer to final copies on the form provided. Address and check envelopes. Mail letters and have students share responses as they arrive.

Explorer Reports

Students will add depth to their knowledge of explorers as well as improve their research and writing skills by completing an explorer report. Assign students an explorer to research or have them draw the names out of a hat. Avoid letting students choose or you may have 30 reports on Columbus. Select explorers with your available resources in mind. It is fine to have more than one person researching the same explorer.

Provide working copies of the forms for the report. For final presentation use forms copied on parchment or linen paper. Share as oral reports. Bind a second copy into a classroom book.

Native American Legends

Native American legends tell about the creation of the world or explain natural events such as how animals got their features. They describe adventures of people and spirits, tribal traditions, and how people got their names.

Begin by reading legends aloud. Discuss how they solve a problem. Have students select main characters for their own legends. Legend settings should reflect Indian groups they have studied. Choose a problem to be solved by the main character and an animal or spirit to help. Stress that they are able to talk to each other. Try three possible solutions. Two fail and the third succeeds. You may want to have students write about how they got their names. Illustrate legends and share with another class or bind into a book for your school resource center.

LETTERS TO REPRESENTATIVES

My Explorer Report About...

Use an encyclopedia and other books to help you answer these questions. Use complete sentences and proofread your work.

1. What is your explorer's full name? _____

_____

2. When was your explorer born? _____

_____

3. Where was your explorer born? _____

_____

4. Describe your explorer's early life. _____

_____

_____

_____

5. For what country or countries did your explorer sail? _____

_____

6. Where and when did your explorer sail? _____

_____

7. Tell about his explorations. _____

_____

_____

_____

_____

8. Why do we still remember your explorer today? _____

_____

_____

_____

9. Complete these sentences.

One interesting thing I learned about _____

was _____

_____

_____

Another interesting thing about _____ was _____

_____

_____

But the most interesting thing of all about _____ was

_____

_____

_____

BIBLIOGRAPHY:

Name of encyclopedia, name of article, volume, page number

_____

_____

Author, name of book, date, page number

1. _____

_____

2. _____

_____

★ Draw a map of your explorer's route or a flag of his country.

★ Use another piece of paper. You may do both a map and a flag!

NATIVE AMERICAN LEGEND

Social Studies Activities

Classroom Tipi

A classroom tipi is a popular "quiet place" that can be easily made for any classroom. You will need six poles or 2 × 2's about 10 feet long. Lash firmly together at the top to form the framework. Two or three old white sheets dyed tan or brown make up the outside covering that is draped over the poles and stapled to hold them securely. Native American designs can be colored on the sheets using colorful permanent marking pens. The tipi can be used year after year as a place for several children to work together on assignments, or quietly read collections of Native American stories gathered from the library and kept inside the tipi.

Cross-Stitch Samplers

Children of long ago often made cross-stitch samplers when they were first learning needlework skills. Show the students pictures from books of old alphabet samplers. Be sure to point out the very young age of the children making the samplers. Have students design a small, simple figure sampler of their own. Give each child a piece of graph paper. Fold the graph paper into fourths to find the center. Mark the center with a pencil and begin the figure working from the center out and putting an "X" in each square used. To transfer the grid paper figure onto fabric, you will need first to choose an even fabric where the thread inter-

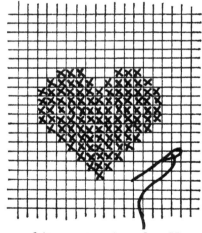

sections show clearly. The material should be ecru, white, or tan in color. You will also need a tapestry needle and embroidery floss for each child. Find the center of the fabric by folding. Mark the center with a pin. Using your grid paper drawing as a guide, count and cross-stitch the drawing onto the fabric—again working from the center to the outside. To make the completed cross-stitch look "old", tea dye with 3-4 tea bags in a mixing bowl of boiling water. Allow the water to cool and put in the cross-stitch. Rinse and wrap in a towel. Do not wring it out. Press the cross-stitch piece with a warm iron on the back side until dry. Frame as desired.

Johnnycakes

Johnnycakes are sometimes called "journey cakes" because they could be make quickly over an open fire or on a small stove in a pioneer cabin.

You will need:
1¹/₂ cups of flour
1¹/₂ cups of cornmeal
1 teaspoon baking powder
¹/₂ teaspoon salt
¹/₂cup shortening
1 tablespoon sugar
3 eggs
1 cup milk

Directions:
1. sift flour, cormeal, baking powder and salt.
2. Beat shortening and sugar with a wooden spoon. Add eggs one at a time.
3. Add flour and milk alternately.
4. Heat a large greased griddle. Drop batter by large spoonfulls onto griddle. Cook to golden on both sides.

Serve your Johnnycakes warm with butter. They also taste good with maple syrup or jam.

Indian Frybread

This modern version of Native American Frybread can easily be made in most classrooms. Students can do most of the work, but you will probably want to do the actual frying yourself.

You will need:
2 cups flour
1 teaspoon salt
2 teaspoons baking powder
¹/₂ cup powdered milk
1 tablespoon sugar
1 cup warm water

Directions:
1. Mix all ingredients together.
2. Knead the dough slightly
3. On a floured board, pat dough into small circles about ¹/₂-inch thick.
4. Fry quickly in hot oil. Cook until nicely browned. Drain on paper towel.

Serve your frybread with homemade butter (below) and jam or honey.

Quick Homemade Butter

Pour one pint of heavy whipping cream into a one quart glass jar. Secure lid tightly. Have students take turns shaking until cream separates. Pour off the liquid. Add a pinch of salt and stir. Refrigerate until firm.

Tin Punching

You can make a simple tin punch lantern from a tin can. You will also need nails, a small hammer, plasticene, an old towel, and a shallow dish pan.

Fill the can with water and freeze until solid. The ice will keep the can from flattening when punched. Work on the floor or a very sturdy table. Place the frozen can on a folded towel inside a shallow dish pan.

With the hammer and a nail punch holes in the can. Create a picture or design with the holes. Use different size nails for larger or smaller holes. Do not make holes in the bottom of the can.

Near the top rim of the can punch two large nail holes on opposite sides. Use a wire hooked through these holes for the lantern's handle. Carefully anchor a small candle inside the lantern with plasticene to finish your project.

For an antique finish on the outside of your lantern, paint with black metal paint (matt finish works best). When the paint is dry, buff with fine steel wool to remove most of the paint. Finish with a coat of clear acrylic.

Historical News

Historical events will come alive for your students if they think of them as news. Have students write stories about historic events as if they were reporting for the six o'clock news. Discuss news stories and how they are written. Stress *who, what, when, where,* and *why.* Include interesting facts and details. Your program may cover a wide range of events or be confined to a single event or brief historical period.

Allow for imagination. How about a weather report from Valley Forge? An interview with an eye witness from Ford's Theater or a live update with Lewis and Clark from the mouth of the Columbia?

Put stories in an interesting order. Use news anchors to introduce and set each scene. Student correspondents tell their own stories of history. Video tape or perform before a live audience.

Sharing Our Heritage

Most families who live in our country now originally came from other parts of the world. Have each child choose a relative or friend who has immigrated or settled in our country. Create a worksheet for students to complete with the help of their parents that tells about the person they have chosen. Include on the worksheet the name of the person, their birthdate, place of birth, when they came to our country, how old the person was when they arrived, where they settled, etc. If the person is still living, how old are they now? If they are no longer living, how old were they when they died? As students return their worksheets, share this rich history on a world map in the classroom by marking the places of birth. Culminate this activity with a food tasting from the various countries. Have each student bring enough small bite sized pieces (one for each member of the class) of a food that represents the native country of the person they have chosen. If possible, have the students include the recipe that they have shared. These recipes could then be included in a "Heritage" or "Cultural Awareness" cookbook.

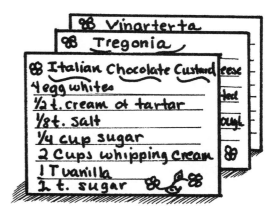

City Box Reports

For this partner research report, each pair of children are to choose a city anywhere in the world and prepare a report on that city. The report should include basic information about location, population, climate, government, history, trade, and industry, etc. Student partners will need to bring from home a box approximately 10 inches wide by 14 inches tall. Cover the box with colorful paper. The student reports can be glued to the side panels of the box. Blank panels may be used for a colored world map showing the city's location, the flag or seal of the state or country, and pictures of special places to visit in their chosen city. Stacked box reports make an interesting, colorful display for the classroom or library.

Wrapping Up Native Americans

There are a wide variety of activities to choose from to wrap up the study of Native Americans. In most areas there are field trips available to visit local museums with Native American exhibits. If this is not possible, consider inviting a guest speaker from a local Native American group to come and speak to your classroom about the history and traditions of their culture. Often they can bring samples of clothing and art work for students to see. Story tellers will often come and present legends to small classroom groups. Within the classroom, students can share the legends they have written, their picture writing, and art projects with younger students or invited parents. Foods such as the Fry Bread recipe included in this book, can be made and served. Awards run on colorful astrobright tagboard can be presented to each student.

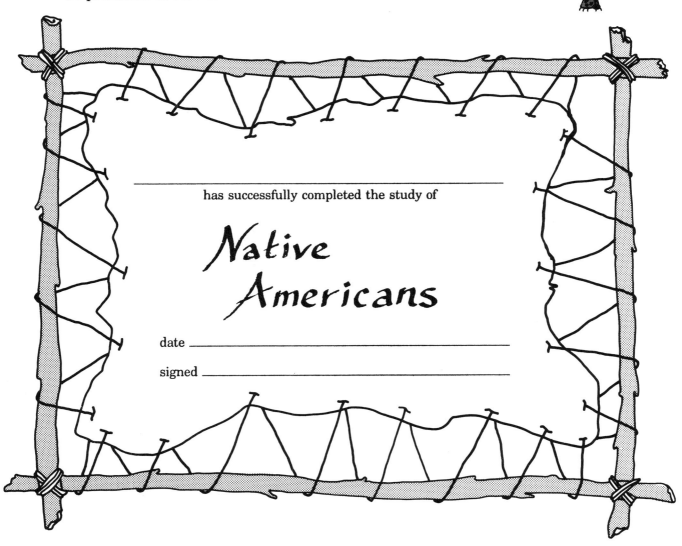

has successfully completed the study of

Native Americans

date _____

signed _____

Wrapping Up American Heritage

Upon completion of the Heritage social studies units, you will have a collection of student writing activities, videos, posters, and art projects. Gathered together they make an interesting display of student work. Invite guests to visit the classroom as students share letters from their representatives, video presentations, and explorer reports, view dioramas, and art projects including tin punch designs, cross-stitch samplers, and their patchwork quilt designs. With students' cooking for their guests, serve Johnnycakes with butter and jam after they have shared their work. This special treat always makes the occasion memorable. Special guests might be students from one grade level below your class. It lets them know about some of the projects they will have to look forward to next year.

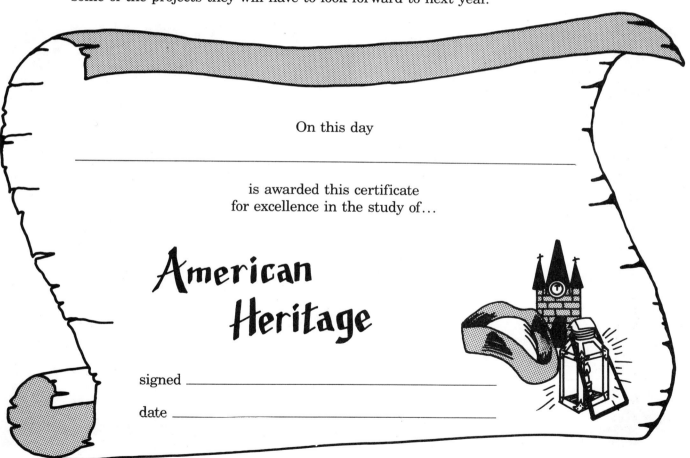

On this day

_____

is awarded this certificate
for excellence in the study of...

American Heritage

signed _____

date _____

Wrapping Up World Regions

Display the City Box Reports in the library or classroom. Have each student tell about the city they choose for their box report. Prepare tagboard city names ahead of time and have each student pin up their city name on a world map. Ask people from the community who have visited various countries to come and share their travel experiences and pictures. Conclude activities with a food tasting party. Foods from the Tropical region are especially appropriate. Most large stores now carry coconuts, kiwi fruit, pineapple, sugarcane, etc., year round. If students made Cultural Awareness Cookbooks, finished copies along with award certificates can be proudly shared with family and friends.

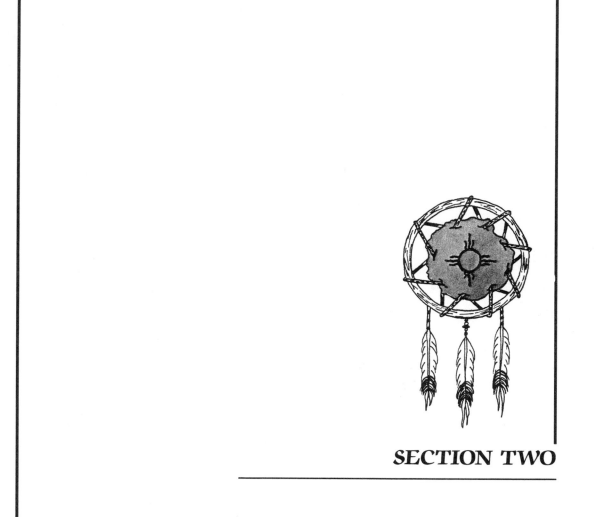

SECTION TWO

NATIVE AMERICANS

Name _____

Look for each of these Native American Tribes in the word search. The names can be found either across or down.

CHEROKEE

SEMINOLE

IROQUOIS

COMANCHE

CHEYENNE

SIOUX

PUEBLO

APACHE

NAVAJO

CHINOOK

NEZ PERCE

SALISH

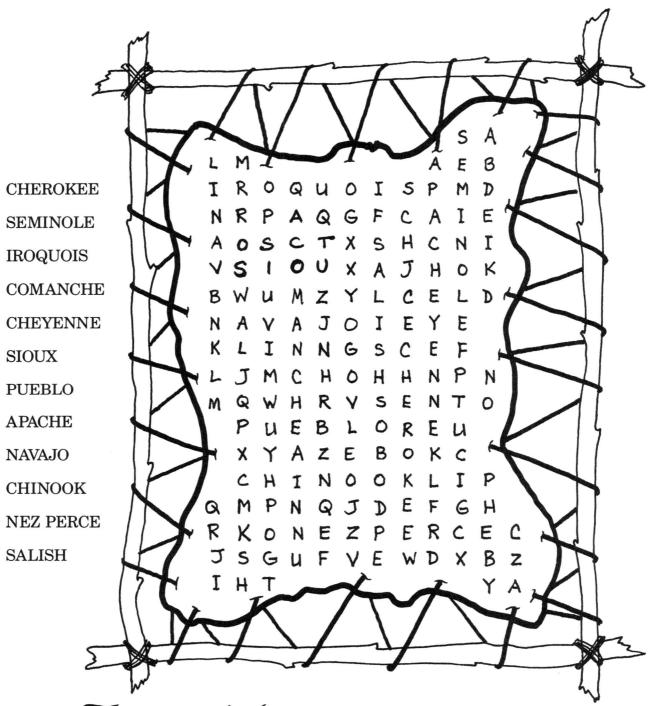

Tribes Word Search

Indian Regions

The story of the American Indian began more than 20,000 years ago. During this time the earth was much different than it is today. Many parts of the earth's surface that are now covered by water, were then dry land. Archaeologists believe that the Indians came to North America from Asia by simply walking across the Bering Strait. They were following herds of animals in search of food. Today the Bering Strait is a 50-mile wide body of water that separates Asia and Alaska.

By the time European explorers came to America, thousands of years had passed and the Indians had made their homes throughout North America. They had settled into four regions; the Woodland Indians, the Plains Indians, the Desert Indians, and the Coastal Indians. These groups were called culture areas. Each group was unique and special, and yet they were alike in many ways.

The Woodland Indians lived in the region that stretches from the border of Canada to the Gulf of Mexico, and from the Mississippi River to the east coast and the Atlantic Ocean. They were farmers, woodsmen, and hunters.

The Plains Indian culture group lived in the region between the Mississippi River and the Rocky Mountains, from Canada to Mexico. They were farmers, fishermen, hunters, and gatherers.

The Desert Indian group lived in what is now the southwestern part of the United States. They were villagers, farmers, and nomads or wanderers who lived by hunting.

The Coastal Indian culture group lived along the forest region from what is now Alaska to northern California and from the Pacific Ocean to the Rocky Mountains. They had plentiful supplies of food and were hunters, gatherers and fishermen.

Using the map as a guide, color each of the four Indian Regions. Using the compass directions complete each of these sentences:

The Coastal Indians lived on the _____ coast.

The Woodland Indians lived on the _____ coast.

The Plains Indians lived _____ of the Woodland Indians.

The Desert Indians lived _____ of the Coastal Indians.

Which Indian group lives nearest to you? _____

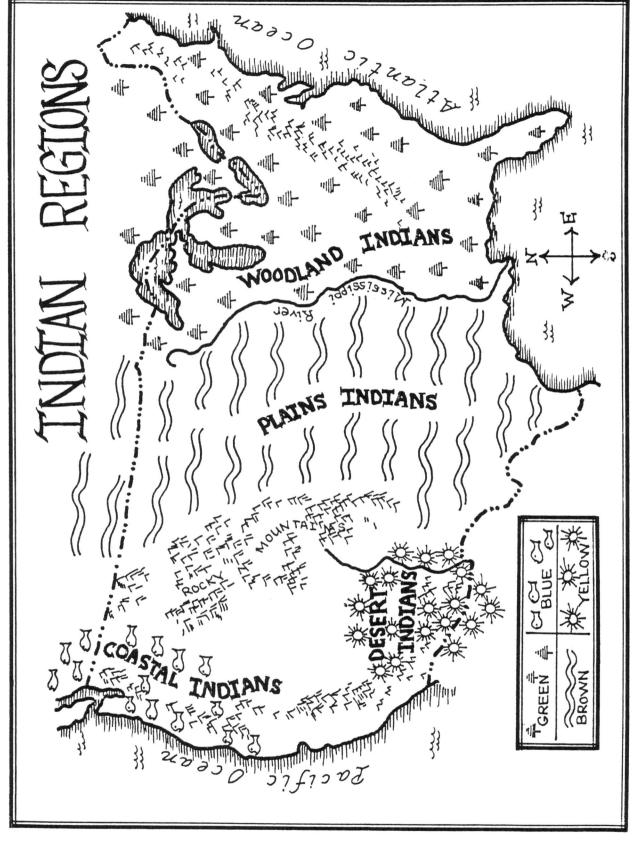

INDIAN REGIONS

WOODLAND INDIANS

PLAINS INDIANS

ROCKY MOUNTAINS

COASTAL INDIANS

DESERT INDIANS

Atlantic Ocean

Pacific Ocean

Mississippi River

N
E
W
S

GREEN
BLUE
YELLOW
BROWN

Name _____

Woodland Indians Handwriting

The Woodland Indians were the first to meet European settlers.

wigwams _____

longhouse _____

moccasins _____

Sequoya _____

birchbark _____

Seminole _____

Iroquois _____

dugout _____

Woodland _____

Pilgrims _____

Name _____

Indians and Pilgrims

As you read this story, circle the correct word in each numbered box at the bottom of the page.

When the Pilgrims first landed in Plymouth Massachusetts in 1620, they were 1._____ by tribes of Woodland Indians who lived peacefully along the coast.

These Indians were used to 2._____ whatever they had with each other. When the Pilgrims arrived, they offered to share with them. If these Indians had not been so kind, the Pilgrims 3._____ not have been able to survive.

During the first year the Pilgrims were at Plymouth, they had 4._____ problems. They were not prepared for the hardships of living in a new land. There was a 5._____ of food. Almost half of the Pilgrims became ill and died during the winter.

The Woodland Indians taught the Pilgrims dozens of 6._____ needed for survival. They taught the Pilgrims how to hunt 7._____ plant corn using fish for fertilizer. They showed the Pilgrims plants that 8._____ be used as medicine. They taught them how to dig and cook clams, and how to get sap from the maple 9._____

In the fall the Pilgrims decided to have a 10._____ to celebrate their good fortune in this new land. The Indians were invited to this feast which we now know and celebrate as Thanksgiving.

1.	2.	3.	4.	5.
captured	sharing	did	many	plenty
met	taking	will	only	shortage
watched	holding	might	never	enough
6.	7.	8.	9.	10.
games	still	could	trees	house
skills	yet	won't	bushes	canoe
work	and	should	syrup	feast

Name _____

Animal Skin Clothing

 **Ready:**

repeated
tanned
embers
buckskin
velvet
breech-clout
fringed
moccasins
embroider
quills

1. _____ are low burning or smoldering coals of a fire.

2. To decorate or stitch with ornamental needlework in designs and patterns is to_____ .

3. An animal hide that has been changed into leather by heating and smoking is said to have been_____ .

4. _____ is a thick, soft cloth fabric.

5. A word that rhymes with "singed" and means to have a rough cut edge is_____ .

6. Something that is done over and over again is_____ .

 Set:

The Woodland Indians wore clothing made from animal skins and fur. Children wore clothing made from the skins of young deer called fawns. Adults wore clothing made from the skins of deer, elk and moose.

Preparing the animal hide for making clothing was a long, hard job. It was done mostly by the women after the men had skinned the animals. First the skin was soaked in water for several days to soften it and make it easier to work with. The skin was taken from the water, wrung out, and laid over a log. Then, the women used sharp-edged stones to scrape off the hair and fat. This soaking and scraping was repeated until all the hair and fat were removed and the skin was smooth and soft.

Next, the animal skin was tanned by heating and smoking it over low burning fire embers. Smoking the skin gave it a warm tan color and protected it from being eaten by moths. Tanned deer hide is called "buckskin." After smoking, the skin was stretched on a pole frame and scraped again until it was as soft as velvet. Only then was the skin ready to be made into clothing.

The men of the Woodland Indian tribes usually wore only a breech-clout. A breech-clout was a length of deerskin looped over a leather cord or belt in back and in front. The women wore leather wrap-around skirts or dresses made of deerskin with fringed edges. Leggings, capes, and moccasins made from animal skins were worn by men, women, and children for protection from the cold during winter months. Often the Woodland Indian women would embroider designs on their moccasins and dresses. To make the designs, they stitched on dyed porcupine quills and beads using bone needles and moose hair thread.

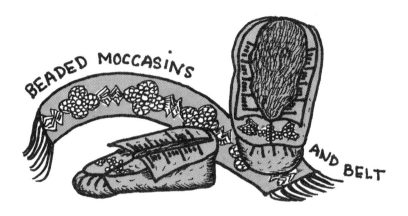

 *Go:*

1. Another name for a young deer is a_____ .

2. The men used sharp-edged stones to scrape the hair and fat from the animal hides. True or False (Circle one)

3. What is buckskin? elk skin, tanned deer hide, or moose hide (circle one)

4. Tanning the hide protected it from being eaten by_____ . What do we use today that does the same thing?_____

5. Who wore breech-clouts? women, men, or children (circle one)

6. What kind of needles were used to embroider on the clothing? _____ What kind of hair was used as thread?_____

Name _____

Woodland Canoes

As you read this story, circle the correct word in each numbered box at the bottom of the page.

The Woodland Indians used dugout canoes and birch 1._____ canoes for fishing and transportation. Dugout canoes were made by hollowing out large trees.

These heavy canoes could 2._____ from 10 to 15 men. Smaller lightweight canoes were made out of birch bark.

To learn about how birch bark canoes were made, we need to 3._____ more about birch trees. The birch tree used for making birch bark canoes is called the "Paper Birch" or "White Birch." Sometimes it is also called "Canoe Birch." The Paper Birch 4._____ to be from 60 to 80 feet tall. The bark from these trees grows in horizontal sheet-like layers. A 5._____ birch tree may have as many as nine layers of bark.

In the springtime when the birch trees are moist and pliable, they are 6._____ down. The bark is carefully peeled off 7._____ large sheets. The outside layers of bark are thick and white. Thinner brownish colored layers are 8._____ . After the bark is peeled, it is shaped, *dark side out,* over a hardwood canoe frame. It is sewn together 9._____ spruce tree roots. Then it is allowed to dry and is sealed with pine tree gum to 10._____ it water water tight.

1.	2.	3.	4.	5.
dirt	weight	listen	grows	small
skin	hold	see	planted	strong
bark	lift	know	falls	large
6.	7.	8.	9.	10.
pushed	with	inside	because	carry
cut	in	under	into	make
bent	beside	near	with	float

Wigwams and Longhouses

 *Ready:*

wigwam
sheltered
sapling
slab
overlapping
compartment
platform
aisle
framework
hearth

1. A two syllable word that names a kind of Woodland Indian home is a _____ .

2. A compound word that means a raised wood floor would be a _____ .

3. A word that has the same beginning sounds as the word heart is_____ .

4. Another name for a young tree is_____ .

5. A thick piece or chunk of something is a _____ .

6. A space partitioned off from the rest of a building is called a _____ .

 *Set:*

The Woodland Indians had two different kinds of homes. The kind of home they lived in depended on the location of their tribe and the kinds of trees available for building homes.

One kind of Woodland Indian home was the wigwam. Wigwams were dome or cone-shaped homes. The framework for the wigwam was made of young green saplings stuck into the ground. These sapling poles were bent inward and tied together at the top. This framework was covered with overlapping sheets of birch bark or woven cattail mats. An animal hide was often hung over the doorway as protection from the cold weather in the winter. In the summer, the cattail mats could be rolled up to let in light and cool air. Inside the wigwams had hard packed dirt floors and raised wooden platforms built for sleeping.

Not all Woodland Indians lived in wigwams. Some lived in long rectangular homes called longhouses. The Indians who lived in longhouses lived in areas where there were very few birch trees. Their longhouses were made of a pole framework that was covered with large slabs of rough elm bark. While the wigwam was usually a home for just one family, the longhouse was the home of many families. A longhouse was about 20 feet wide and 120 feet long. An aisle and fire hearths were located in the center of the longhouse. Each family lived in sheltered compartments facing each other. The aisle and fire hearth separated the families. As many as 20 families might live together in one longhouse.

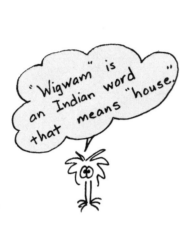

"Wigwam" is an Indian word that means "house."

 Go:

1. Name two kinds of Woodland Indian homes._____ and_____

2. To make a wigwam, the saplings must be bent (outward, inward, or sideways)

3. Name two things that were used to cover the outside of a wigwam.

_____ and _____

4. A longhouse was a home for one family. Yes _____ or No _____

5. Where were the fireplaces located in a longhouse? _____

6. Which kind of Woodland Indian home was rectangular in shape? _____

7. What shape was a wigwam, (cone, square, or round)

Sequoya's Alphabet

For hundreds of years the Indians of North America had no written language. Then, in 1821, a Cherokee Indian man named Sequoya invented a way of writing symbols for the sounds of his language. Sequoya did this without knowing how to read or write. He began by breaking spoken words into syllables. He discovered that there were 86 different sounds in the Cherokee language. He created a symbol to represent each sound. Some of the symbols he made up. Other symbols he borrowed from our alphabet that we use today. By putting the symbols together, Sequoya was able to make words that could be written down and read by others.

1. LOOK AT THE CHEROKEE WRITING BELOW.
2. WRITE THE MEANING UNDER EACH PICTURE.
3. NUMBER THE PICTURES IN THE CORRECT ORDER.
4. CUT OUT THE PICTURES AND GLUE THEM ON ANOTHER SHEET OF PAPER IN THE CORRECT ORDER.

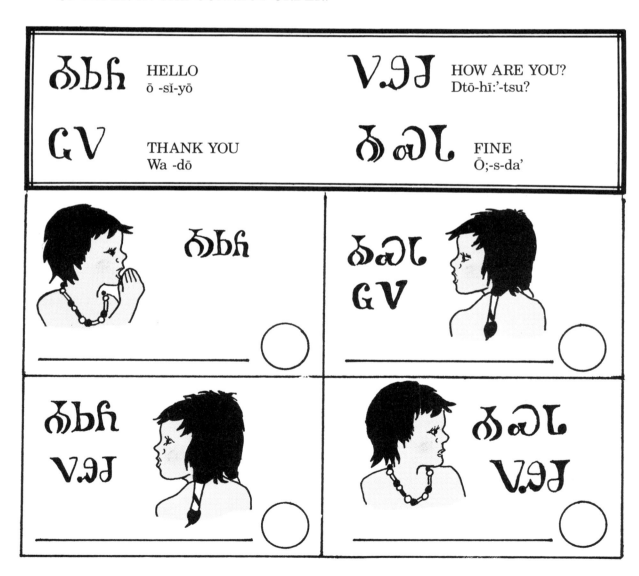

Name _____

"The Dish" Game Math

Woodland Indian children liked to play a game called "The Dish." This game was played with six plum seeds. The seeds were smoothed and flattened so that they looked like buttons. The seeds were painted black on one side and white on the other side.

To play the game the players made a "pot" of one hundred dried beans. The plum seeds were put into a wooden bowl and tossed into the air. When the seeds landed on the ground, points were scored. If all six seeds came down the same color, the player took 20 beans from the "pot" and took another turn. If five seeds came down the same color, the player took 2 beans from the "pot" and took another turn. If only three or four seeds came down the same color, the player lost his turn and passed the seeds to the next player. The game ended when all the beans were gone from the "pot." The player with the most beans at the end of the game was the winner. You can make and play "The Dish" game yourself using buttons or coins instead of plum seeds.

FOUR CHILDREN PLAYED THE DISH GAME BELOW. LOOK AT THEIR SCORES AND SEE IF YOU CAN FIND OUT WHO WON THE GAME.

Bright Star	Lone Wolf	Falling Star	Little Beaver

1. Circle groups of 20 beans for each player.

2. How many groups of 20 beans did you find for the four players? _____

3. Which player had the highest score? _____

4. Which player had the lowest score? _____

5. Write in the total score for all four players. _____

6. Was Bright Star's score greater than or less than Little Beaver's score? _____

★*BONUS* If Bright Star and Lone Wolf played as partners against Falling Star and Little Beaver, who would have won the game? _____

Name _____

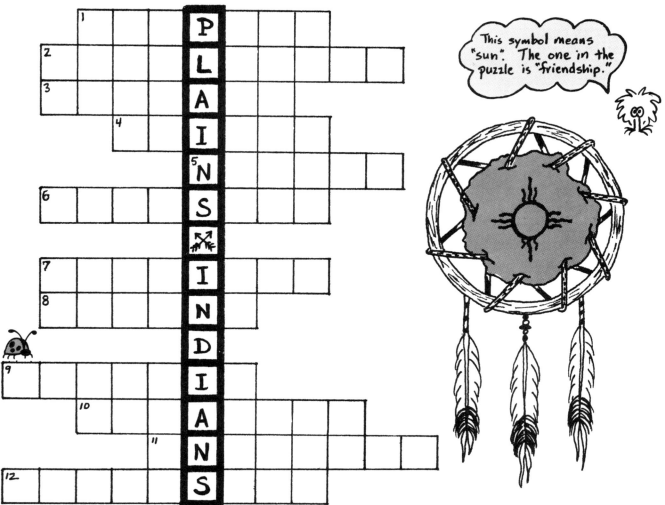

This symbol means "sun". The one in the puzzle is "friendship."

The vertical word in the puzzle is: P L A I N S I N D I A N S

Clues:

1. cone-shaped skin tents
2. Indian "suitcases"
3. bison
4. Indian groups
5. people living without permanent homes
6. soft leather used for clothing
7. dried meat
8. grass lands
9. type of sled for hauling
10. kind of weapon
11. quick, deerlike animal
12. shoes made of buffalo hide

coup
pemmican
antelope
travois
plains
moccasins
teepee
nomads
buckskin
tribes
ceremony
tomahawk
buffalo
parfleches

Plains Indian Tipis

As you read this story, circle the correct word in each numbered box at the bottom of this sheet.

The Plains Indians were nomad hunters. Much of the year they 1._____ in temporary homes that could be carried easily as they followed the buffalo in search of food. Their 2._____ were called tipis.

A tipi looks like a cone-shaped tent with a bare 3._____ floor. To build a tipi, slender lodge pole pines were lashed and interlocked 4._____ to form a frame. This frame was covered with buffalo cowskins that were 5._____ over the poles. The hides were pegged down at the base and 6._____ together with wooden pins. The top of the tipi had smoke flaps to control the smoke from the fire inside. Designs and symbols were painted by the men to decorate the 7._____ of the hides.

An average-sized tipi, big enough to house a family of eight, was about 18 feet high and 14 feet across. A tipi this size would 8._____ 10 to 12 buffalo hides covering the frame. Setting up and taking 9._____ of the tipi was the women's job.

The women could 10._____ up a tipi in about 15 minutes and take it down in less than 3 minutes!

Some people spell it "teepee", but "tipi" is correct... ..."ti" means "dwelling" and "pi" means "used for."

1.	2.	3.	4.	5.
worked lived traveled	homes places person	wood soiled earth	together near careful	stiff caught stretched
6.	7.	8.	9.	10.
joined loose skin	over outside under	have been straight	up over down	set down escape

All About the Buffalo

 *Ready:*

roamed
utensils
pemmican
tendons
jerky
surround
survived
moccasins
stampeding
herds

1. A kind of shoes worn by the Plains Indians would be_____ .

2. A person who has traveled or wandered has_____ .

3. If you enclose something on all sides you_____ it.

4. _____ is a dried meat paste made into cakes.

5. "Words" rhymes with _____ .

6. Spoons, forks, and knives are_____ used for eating food.

Set:

Many years ago great herds of buffalo roamed the plains area in search of food. These herds of buffalo were followed and hunted by the Plains Indians. The buffalo gave the Plains Indians everything they needed to survive.

The meat of the buffalo was not the only part of the buffalo important to the Plains Indians. Every part of the buffalo was used for something. The hides were used for clothing, moccasins, and coverings for tipis. Spoons and other utensils were made from the horns and bones. The hair was used to make rope. The muscles and tendons were dried and used as string and thread. Even the stomach was used as a pot for carrying and cooking food and water.

The Plains Indians had several ways of killing the buffalo. One way was to chase the buffalo on horses and kill it with bows and arrows. The other way was to surround the buffalo and drive them stampeding over the steep cliffs to be killed on the rocks below.

Bullboats made of buffalo skins were used to cross rivers.

The Plains Indians killed only the buffalo they needed. They never killed more than they could use. After killing the buffalo, the Indians would skin it, cut up the meat, and carry it back to their camp. The meat was shared by everyone. Meat that was not eaten right away was dried in the sun or over smoking fires. The women then pounded the dry meat with stones. They mixed it with buffalo fat and dried berries. This was called pemmican. Pemmican would last for many months and was saved to feed the tribes during the cold winter months. The Plains Indians often took pemmican on their buffalo hunting trips much like you might take beef jerky with you on a camping trip.

 Go:

1. What animal gave the Plains Indians everything that they needed to survive?____

2. Tell two ways that the Plains Indians killed buffalo.

_____

_____

3. Pounded buffalo meat, buffalo fat, and dried berries make_____.

4. Clothing, moccasins, and tipis were made from buffalo hides.   Yes   No

5. What food do we eat today that is like pemmican?_____

6. Why do you think there are very few buffalo alive today?_____

_____

The Travois

As you read this story, circle the correct word in each numbered box at the bottom of this sheet.

Strange as it may seem to us

1._____ , the Indians of long ago did not have wheels to use for moving things from place to place. Anything they wanted to

2._____ had to be either carried in bundles or skin sacks, or dragged on what was called a travois.

A travois was 3._____ with two long slender pine poles. These poles were lashed

together at the top and spread 4._____ at the bottom so that they looked like the letter

A. Buffalo hide was stretched and tied between the poles to 5._____ a platform. The load being carried was fastened to the platform. The bottom lower ends of the travois poles

dragged 6._____ the ground.

The early Plains Indians used the travois to 7._____ their tipi poles and buffalo

hides. The travois was pulled by a dog. A strong dog could 8._____ about 75 pounds.

Later, after horses were brought to the Plains, they were used to pull the 9._____ . A

horse pulled travois could carry over 300 pounds

and could travel 10._____ as far as a
dog each day.

© 1989 by The Center for Applied Research in Education, Inc.

1.	2.	3.	4.	5.
today	plant	bought	apart	divide
yesterday	protect	cleaned	near	make
tomorrow	move	built	close	separate
6.	7.	8.	9.	10.
with	hide	carry	buffalo	not
along	cover	drop	hides	twice
stumble	carry	eat	travois	never

Name _____

Picture Writing

There were many different tribes of Indians living on the Great Plains. Each tribe had its own spoken language. These tribes often moved from place to place and found other people speaking languages that they did not understand. To understand and communicate with each other, they used sign language and picture writing.

In sign language, the Plains Indians moved their hands and fingers in certain ways to make signs that other Indian tribes understood. In picture writing, the Plains Indians used small drawn symbols that stood for words and ideas. Picture writing was used to decorate their homes and often painted on buffalo hides to record important events in the life of the tribe. Usually, stories were written in a circle instead of on lines like we use for writing.

On the lower part of this page are some Plains Indian symbols that were used in picture writing. Look at them carefully to see what each symbol means. Then, on the next page try to write your own picture story. Remember the "little words" we use every day are not written. The pictures tell the story.

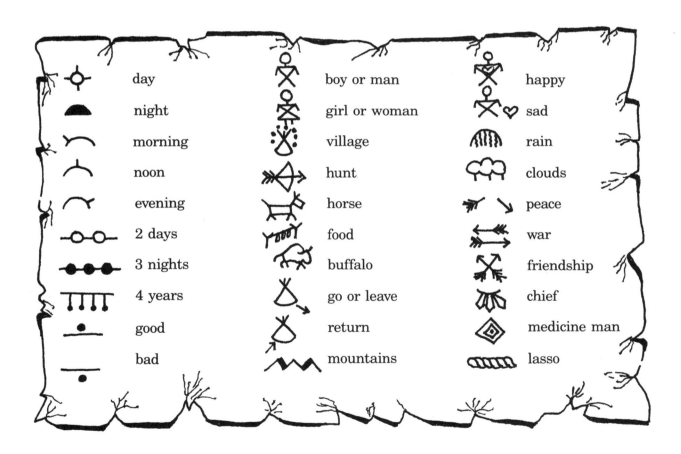

day	boy or man	happy
night	girl or woman	sad
morning	village	rain
noon	hunt	clouds
evening	horse	peace
2 days	food	war
3 nights	buffalo	friendship
4 years	go or leave	chief
good	return	medicine man
bad	mountains	lasso

Write your own story on the buffalo hide below.

Picture Writing Stories

Can you write a story in a circle?

Name _____

Sacajawea

As you read this story, circle the correct word in each numbered box at the bottom of this page.

Sacajawea was a famous Plains Indian woman. She was 1._____ in the late 1780's and was a member of the Shoshone tribe. Her name, Sacajawea, meant "Bird Woman."

When Sacajawea was a 2._____ she was captured and traded by enemy Indians. When she grew older, she was sold to a French fur trader named Charbonneau and 3._____ became his wife.

In 1804, two explorers named Meriwether Lewis and William Clark, set out from St. Louis, Missouri to 4._____ and map the country across the Rocky Mountains to the 5._____ Ocean. Lewis and Clark hired the fur trader Charbonneau and Sacajawea to be guides and interpreters 6._____ the journey.

Sacajawea was an important member of the Lewis and Clark Expedition. She knew the mountain 7._____ and could speak the languages of many of the tribes. Lewis and Clark knew that they would meet the Shoshone Indians when they crossed the Rocky Mountains. For them, Sacajawea was a sign of peace as she helped the Indians to 8._____ that Lewis and Clark were friendly. Sacajawea guided the expedition along the way 9._____ her two month old son "Pompey" on her back! They crossed the Rocky Mountains, went down the Columbia River, and were the first explorers to 10._____ the Pacific Ocean traveling west by land.

1.	2.	3.	4.	5.
born lived part	trader explorer child	later often seldom	dig study walk	Pacific Arctic Atlantic
6.	7.	8.	9.	10.
inside over on	trails peaks steep	care wish understand	putting carrying laying	reach cover lose

Parfleche

The Plains Indians and some other Indian groups used a parfleche to carry some of their treasured possessions and dried food. These parfleches were made from waterproof rawhide which was folded in a special way to make a sealed envelope. Often dried strips of meat, dried peppermint, and dried berries were carried inside a parfleche to keep them from spoiling. The women drew geometric designs on the outside of the parfleches. They painted these designs with softened buffalo bone brushes.

 Using a separate sheet of paper, see if you can follow the directions below and make a parfleche for yourself.

 You Will Need These Materials:

A piece of 8½ by 11 inch tan colored paper
A 24-inch piece of colored braided yarn
that has been tied at both ends
Red, yellow, and blue marking pens

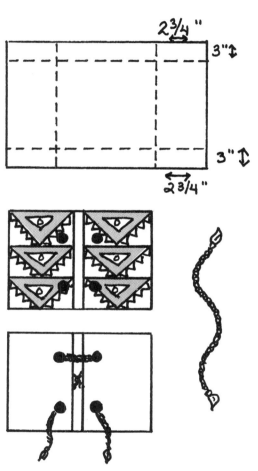

 **Follow These Directions:**

Mark your paper using a ruler
Fold your paper along the lines

Carefully punch the 4 holes
Decorate with geometric designs

Draw your yarn through the top holes
Cross the yarn on the inside
Tie a bow on the outside

Another Way to Make a Parfleche:

For a more natural looking rawhide parfleche, cut 8½ by 11 inch pieces of brown grocery sack paper. Complete all the measurements and punch the holes. Then *carefully* crumple the paper over and over. It will become soft like rawhide. Continue to fold, decorate, and tie your parfleche.

Name _____

Southwest Indians Handwriting

adobe _____

_____

pueblo _____

_____

hogan _____

_____

kachina _____

_____

kiva _____

_____

maize _____

_____

weaving _____

_____

pottery _____

_____

turquoise _____

_____

sandpainting _____

_____

Name _____

Hogans and Pueblos

 *Ready:*

mesa
sagebrush
climate
hogan
pueblo
adobe
apartment
dwelling
canyon
remains

1. A compound word that is a kind of bush found in desert areas is_____ .

2. Pueblo homes were made from a mixture of straw and clay called _____ .

3. _____ is the kind of weather found in an area.

4. A deep valley with steep sides is a _____ .

5. Something left behind is called _____ .

6. A word that rhymes with "swelling" and means a home where people live is a _____ .

 *Set:*

    The Desert Indians lived in an area where the land was dry and rocky. There were high flat-topped mountains called mesas with steep cliffs and valleys below. There was little rainfall. The land was covered with sagebrush, cactus, and desert plants, but very few trees. Because of the climate, the Desert Indians had to build their homes with whatever materials were available.

    One kind of desert home was called a hogan. A hogan had eight sides and was made of logs. The cracks between the logs were sealed with mud. Grass was often grown on the top of the hogan to keep out the heat in the daytime and the cold at night. The doorway of the hogan faced east toward the rising sun.

    Another kind of Desert Indian home was the pueblo. The name "pueblo" comes from the Spanish word that means "village." The walls of the pueblo were made with stones brought from the desert. These stones were covered and set together with a mixture of desert clay, black river earth, and straw. This mixture, called "adobe," dried smooth and hard in the desert sun. Pueblo homes were often three or four stories high and had as many as two hundred room. They were like apartment houses we have today with many families living together in their own separate rooms.

To protect themselves from their enemies, some of the Desert Indians became cliff dwellers. The cliff dwellers moved their homes stone by stone from the bottom of the canyons to the huge caves in the rocky canyon walls. They chopped steps out of the cliff walls and used ladders to reach from one level to another. These ladders were pulled up at night and when there was danger of attack from other Indians. If you visit the southwestern part of the United States today, you can still see the remains of the pueblos and the cliff dwellers' homes in the steep canyon walls.

 Go:

1. Name two kinds of Desert Indian homes. _____ and _____

2. What is adobe made of? _____

3. The Spanish word for village is (hogan, adobe, or pueblo) Circle one.

4. Cliff dwellers used _____ to reach from one level to another.

5. How many rooms might there be in pueblo homes? (10, 200, or 2,000) _____

6. Can you still find pueblo and cliff dwellings in the southwestern part of the United States today? Yes or No Circle one.

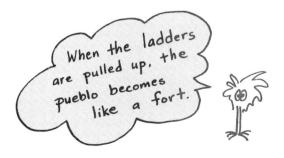

When the ladders are pulled up, the pueblo becomes like a fort.

Name _____

Kachinas

As you read this story, circle the correct word in each numbered box at the bottom of the page.

The Desert Indians of the Southwest believed in friendly spirits called kachinas. Kachina spirits 1._____ in the mountains. They were not gods. They were kind and loving spirits that were go-betweens for the people and nature. The kachinas helped the people 2._____ to live a good life and to respect the beauty and power of nature.

Kachina dolls and dancers were symbols of the kachina spirits. There were over 250 different 3._____ of kachinas. Some were animals, birds, plants, or weather symbols.

Desert Indian people 4._____ that the kachinas looked after the weather and the harvest.

Kachina dolls were carved from cottonwood roots by the men of the tribe. They were painted and 5._____ with bits of shells, feathers and turquoise stones. Kachina dolls were given as 6._____ to children to teach them about the power, love and spirits of the kachinas.

Each year kachina dancers performed rain ceremonies to 7._____ the spirits that rain was needed for their crops. Kachina dancers were men who were trained to 8._____ costumes and masks of the kachinas. A man did not become a kachina spirit, but the spirit was with him during the ceremonies. At the 9._____ of the rain ceremonies, the kachina dancers would often visit the homes of the children. They would ask the children if they had been 10._____ and give them gifts of food.

© 1989 by The Center for Applied Research in Education, Inc.

1.	2.	3.	4.	5.
lived	travel	kinds	wanted	decorated
watching	play	dolls	believed	burned
hoped	learn	spirits	caught	planted
6.	7.	8.	9.	10.
food	remind	dancing	middle	good
warning	know	wear	done	happy
gifts	carry	dress	end	kachina

Name _____

Amazing Maize Maze

The Desert Indians grew what we now call "Indian corn." It was their main crop raised for food. Desert Indian legends say that corn was a gift to the people from the kachinas. The people looked upon corn as if it were a person because it needed to be cared for in order to grow.

Each spring the corn fields were planted in rows at the bottom of the canyons below their pueblo homes. Indian corn did not look like the yellow corn we see today. It grew in many colors—blue, white, yellow, red, pink, and purple. The Desert Indians built dams and dug ditches to bring water to the corn plants.

Most of the corn that was harvested was dried and kept in storerooms or in pits dug outside the pueblo homes. Corn could be used in many ways. Ground cornmeal was used to make tortillas and piki bread. Corn was also used in making soups, stews, and a drink called pasole.

TRACE THE PATH FROM THE KERNEL OF CORN THROUGH THE STALKS TO THE EAR OF CORN.

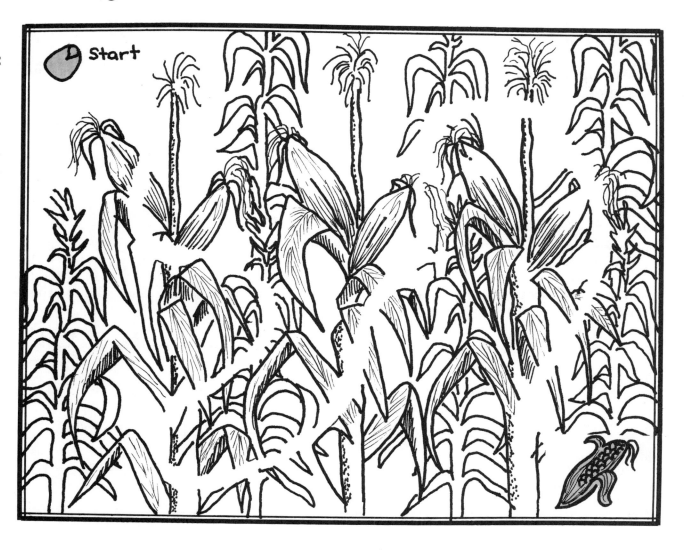

Name _____

The Kiva

As you read this story, circle the correct word in each numbered box at the bottom of the page.

A kiva is like a Desert Indian church building. The kiva was either round or rectangular in 1._____ . Huge kivas were used by everyone in the village. Smaller kivas were used by families. Some kivas were built above the 2._____ and had roofs made of mud and logs. Other kivas were large underground rooms.

According to Indian tradition, young boys were 3._____ to the kiva by their fathers and grandfathers. They were taught the songs, dances, and ceremonies of their people.

Rain was very 4._____ for the survival of the Desert Indians and was part of many events. Often kachina dancers performed ceremonies inside the 5._____ to keep rain falling and their crops growing.

One ceremony, called "Powama" was 6._____ at the end of winter in February. The men planted sprout trays 7._____ bean and corn seeds. The seeds were kept moist and warm by the 8._____ that burned all night inside the kiva. When the new seedlings sprouted, they were taken outside for all of the village people to 9._____ . If the seedlings were healthy, it meant that the summer crops of beans and corn would be good.

The men spent a lot of time in the kiva. It was like a clubhouse for them. They used the kiva as a workshop, for ceremonies, and meetings. Women were 10._____ allowed to go into the kivas except on special occasions.

1. size circle shape	2. ground houses mountains	3. hidden left brought	4. unusual important useless	5. kivas pueblos hogans
6. played performed taught	7. with of because	8. walls dancers fires	9. see catch sprout	10. maybe sometimes not

Name _____

Arts and Crafts

The Desert Indians are famous for their art and craft work. They made a great variety of beautiful pottery pieces, weavings, and jewelry. As you read about each of these art forms, think about how you can use designs of your own on a pottery bowl, a woven blanket, and a piece of jewelry.

Bowls, pots, and jars were made from reddish clay dug from nearby hills or canyon bottoms. After the clay was mixed, it was coiled and shaped. It was dried, sanded, polished, and painted. The designs were painted on with a brush made from the yucca plant. Common designs were geometric shapes, coils, zig-zags, bands, dots, and animal and bird designs. Then the pottery pieces were placed upside down on the ground to be fired. During firing the reddish clay turns black. When the ashes cooled, the pots were dug out and cleaned and were then ready to use.

Blankets, rugs, ponchos, and serapes were woven by the Desert Indians. Raw wool was sheared, washed, dyed, carded, and spun into yarn by hand. The yarn was woven into blankets, rugs and clothing on simple looms set up outside their homes. Each weaver created their own designs, so that no two woven pieces are alike. Geometric designs were woven from the bottom up to the top of the loom. Somewhere in each woven piece there is a break in the design. It is not a mistake. It is an "escape route" for the weaver's spirit. In some cultures only the men were allowed to weave. In other cultures only the women were weavers.

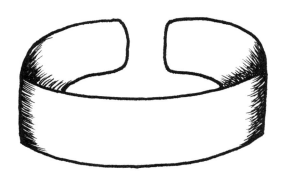

Early Desert Indian jewelry was worn to protect a person from evil. The jewelry was made of turquoise. Turquoise is a blue-green stone found mainly in desert areas. At first the jewelry was made from chips of the turquoise stone glued to wood with pitch and ash. About 1850 the Mexicans introduced silversmithing to the Desert Indians. From that time on the jewelry was made from silver and turquoise. The silver was carefully hammered around the turquoise stone to fasten it together. Special designs were hammered into the silver. Then the piece was shaped into a ring, bracelet, necklace or buckle.

 BELOW ARE SOME DESIGN PATTERNS USED ON POTTERY, WEAVING, AND JEWELRY. USE THESE DESIGN PATTERNS OR SOME OF YOUR OWN TO COMPLETE YOUR OWN BOWL, RUG AND PIECE OF JEWELRY.

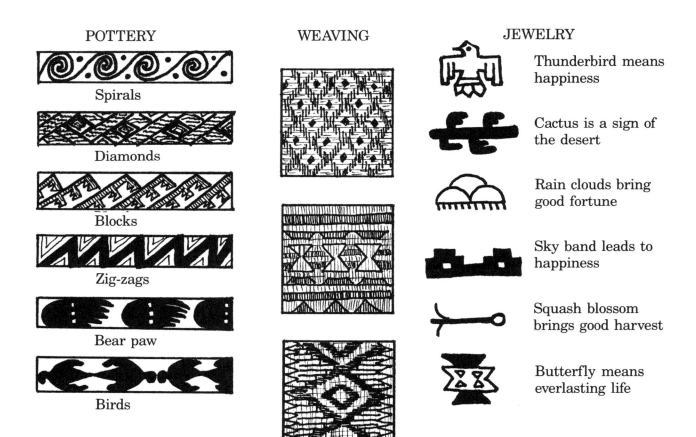

POTTERY

Spirals

Diamonds

Blocks

Zig-zags

Bear paw

Birds

WEAVING

JEWELRY

Thunderbird means happiness

Cactus is a sign of the desert

Rain clouds bring good fortune

Sky band leads to happiness

Squash blossom brings good harvest

Butterfly means everlasting life

Sandpainting Math

Sandpainting is another Desert Indian art form. Long ago sandpainting was done by medicine men as part of healing ceremonies for curing people who were sick. To begin a sandpainting, colored rocks are crushed to make different colored sands. Next, white sand is spread over the floor as a background for the painting. Then, the colored sand is sprinkled slowly from the painter's fingers to make the design. Sandpaintings can be as large as 10 feet across. There are over 10,000 separate designs used. Long ago sandpaintings were started early in the morning and were always destroyed at sunset.

```
1 pint  = 2 cups
1 quart = 2 pints
1 gallon = 4 quarts
```

MOTHER EARTH   **FATHER SKY**

1. The medicine man has made 2 sandpaintings. The sandpainting of Mother Earth used 8 gallons of sand. The sandpainting of Father Sky also used 8 gallons of sand.

   How many gallons of sand were used to make both of the paintings? _____

2. How many quarts of sand were used to make both of the sandpaintings? The chart in the box will help you solve this problem. _____

3. If 8 quarts of the sand used in the 2 sandpaintings were white, how many quarts of the other colored sand were used to make both paintings? The answer to problem number 2 will help you solve this problem. _____

4. Four cups of special red sand was used in the sandpaintings. How many quarts of special red sand were used? _____

"Klahowya Sikhs"

Look at the list of words in the word box. They are words you will learn about as you study the Coastal Indians. Unscramble the letters of each word at the bottom of the page and fill in the word puzzle. One letter for each word has been written for you. When your puzzle is complete, you will have a Chinook Indian greeting.

Blanket
Tribe
Ceremony
Totem
Potlatch
Symbol
Spawn
Coastal
Longhouse
Basket
Honor
Salmon
Canoe

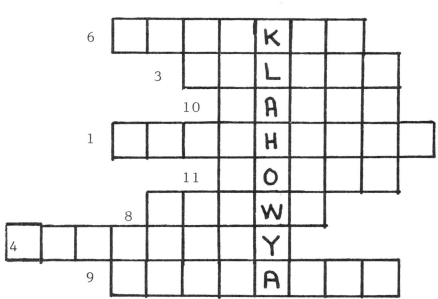

1. HLOONUSGE
2. TSCAOAL
3. NLMAOS
4. NREYOECM
5. SEBKAT
6. ALETBNK
7. NHOOR

8. PWSAN
9. OAHPCTLT
10. AONEC
11. TMEOT
12. BSLMOY
13. ITEBR

KLAHOWYA SIKHS in Chinook jargon means "hello friend".

All About the First Fish

 Ready:

edible
seafood
salmon
special
honor
area
humans
considered
cycle
spawn
guarantee
ceremony

1. Three words in which the "c" has the sound of the letter "s" are _____ , _____ , and _____ .

2. A salt and fresh water fish is a _____ .

3. Fish _____ or lay eggs to produce offspring.

4. If a food is safe to be eaten it is_____ .

5. A four letter word with three syllables is_____ .

6. The word which begins with a silent "h" and means to respect is _____ .

 Set:

The Coastal Indians always had plenty of food nearby to eat. The waters of the coastal area were rich with many kinds of seafood. Coastal Indians ate clams, oysters, halibut, cod, and many other kinds of fish and shellfish. But, the salmon was the Coastal Indians' main food.

The Coastal Indians believed that the salmon were like humans. They believed that the salmon lived in a huge longhouse deep in the Pacific Ocean. Each year these "salmon people" turned themselves from undersea people into fish. Then they were caught by the Indian people with nets, traps and spears.

The first salmon caught each year was considered by the Coastal Indians to be a very special fish. The Indians had a ceremony to honor this first fish. Fern leaves were used to clean it. After the fish was cooked, small pieces of the fish were shared with every man, woman, and child in the village. The heart of the fish was burned in the fire. After the fish had been shared by the village, the bones of the fish were taken to the shores of a nearby river and thrown into the water. The Coastal Indians believed that throwing the fish bones into the river would mean more fish would return the next year. And they always did!

If you read about the life cycle of the salmon, you will learn that the salmon will return from the salt water to spawn or lay its eggs in the same fresh water place year after year. Strange as it may seem, the Coastal Indian's belief in returning the salmon bones to the rivers to guarantee more fish is very much like what the scientists today know happens to the spawning salmon.

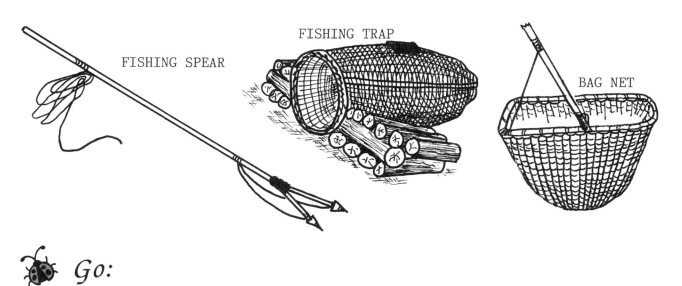

FISHING SPEAR

FISHING TRAP

BAG NET

Go:

1. The main food of the Coastal Indians was _____ .

2. "Salmon people" lived in a big longhouse in the _____ Ocean.

3. The first salmon caught each year was shared by everyone. (Yes, No)

4. Salmon return from salt water to lay their eggs in _____ water.

5. In the story the "salmon people" turn themselves into _____ .

6. The Coastal Indians had a special _____ to honor the first fish that was caught each year.

Name _____

Longhouses

As you read this story, circle the correct word in each numbered box at the bottom of the page.

The Coastal Indians lived along the shores of

1._____ water rivers or near the salt water of Puget Sound and the Pacific Ocean. Their winter

2._____ were called longhouses.
Longhouses were made of large overlapping cedar

planks. They had pointed roofs to 3._____ the rain. Some of the longhouses 4._____ 200 feet long. These homes were so large that several families could live together inside.

There were 5._____ windows in the longhouses. Large fires burned in the middle of

the dirt floor. A hole in the roof allowed the 6._____ from fires to escape. Cedar and cattail mats were hung up to make small rooms for the families. The mats were also

7._____ for rugs and mattresses.

The floor of the longhouse was covered with cedar 8._____ shavings. If the floor got

dirty, the shavings were swept outside and new shavings were 9._____ down on the floor.
The Coastal Indians lived in longhouses from November to April each year. The summer homes of the Coastal Indians were simple lean-tos or huts called cattail

mathouses. The outside was 10._____ with cedar bark mats and cattails. These homes could be easily moved from place to place in the summer as the Indians gathered food to prepare for the next winter.

1. cold warm fresh	2. canoes homes clothing	3. hold catch shed	4. were lasted was	5. near not no
6. chimney smoke air	7. used made taken	8. splinter seeds bark	9. thrown hung gathered	10. under covered nailed

Potlatch Ceremony

The potlatch gift-giving ceremony was the most important social event in the lives of the Coastal Indians. Potlatches were given on special occasions. Usually only wealthy village chiefs gave a potlatch. They gave potlatches to pass on family dances, songs, and chants. Potlatches were also given when someone married, died, or got a new name. Other potlatches were given when the salmon runs began, or after a good hunt. Many chiefs gave potlatches to show others how wealthy they were.

Honor was a very important part of the potlatch. Often a family would work together for several years preparing for a potlatch. They would weave baskets and rugs, carve bowls and create other types of artwork that they would give as gifts to their potlatch guests.

Some potlatches were small and others were large. At a large potlatch whole tribes would come and stay for a week. At the potlatch there was always a big feast. There was singing and dancing on the beach. There were also canoe races and games. On the last day of the potlatch, the guests all went to the chief's house. The wealthiest guests sat closest to the chief. They would have feasting and entertainment. People told stories about the chief's family history. The chief's relatives sang, danced, and acted out stories for the guests. At the end of the last day, the chief gave away his gifts.

If you were invited to a potlatch, you were expected to give a potlatch to repay the gifts that were given to you. To keep your honor, you had to give a gift that was more valuable than the gift you received. If you did not, you would lose your honor.

You have read the story about the Coastal Indian potlatch. You can pretend that you are a guest at a potlatch. Get together with three or four other children. Choose one person to be the chief. Give each person a sheet with pictures of potlatch gifts. Color all of the pictures. Cut out each of the squares. Now you are ready to exchange gifts with the chief. The chief will give you each a gift. Remember that you must give a more valuable gift to the chief. You may need to give more than one gift to equal what the chief gives you.

Potlatch Gifts

BASKET   WOVEN MAT   JEWELRY

FOOD   WOODEN BOX   CANOE

BLANKET   DISHES   SLAVES

Name _____

Canoes

As you read this story, circle the correct word in each numbered box at the bottom of the page.

The Coastal Indians were sometimes called "canoe Indians." Canoes were used as

1._____ for fishing, trading, visiting, and going to war. Shovel nose canoes were small and made to be used for traveling and fishing in rivers. Large, 50 foot-long sharp nose

2._____ were used for whale hunting. They could carry 20 to 30 people and cut easily

through 3._____ ocean waters.

Canoes were made from half of a cedar log. The log was roughly shaped by splitting off

slabs of wood. The inside was hollowed out by 4._____ burning and scraping away the

charred wood. Then, the hollowed-out center was 5._____ with water. Hot rocks were

dumped 6._____ the canoe to warm and soften the wood. Wooden crosspieces were put

in the center of the canoe to 7._____ the sides and make the canoe wide in the middle and narrow at the ends.

After the canoe was stretched and shaped, the water was then dumped 8._____ .

The canoe was allowed to dry. When it was dry, it was sanded to make it 9._____ . The rough dried skin of shark or dogfish was used for sandpaper. When the sanding was

10._____ the Coastal Indians rubbed the canoe inside and out with whale oil to give it a waterproof seal and preserve it. Canoes were kept covered with mats when they were not being used. The Indians knew that if they damaged their canoes, it would take a long time and a lot of hard work to make a new one.

© 1989 by The Center for Applied Research in Education, Inc.

1. housing transportation traveling	2. canoes longhouses trees	3. smooth light rough	4. slowly chopping quickly	5. chilled carried filled
6. out into over	7. close stretch break	8. out underneath into	9. bumpy clean smooth	10. started finished work

Totem Poles

Totem poles were carved out of giant cedar trees by the Northwest Coastal Indians. A totem pole is like a book that you might read. The totem poles were a way of passing stories from one generation to another.

The figures on the totem poles were symbols, usually of animals and birds. They were not worshipped. They represented a tribe, clan, family, or person. Some totem poles told of events that happened to a clan. Other totems told about the history of a family. Still others were memorials carved to mark graves. Having a totem pole was an honor, and often families would trade all of their possessions for the honor of having a pole.

After felling the cedar tree, carvers would begin by carving symbols at the top of the tree and work toward the bottom. A totem pole could be small or large. A large totem pole might be more than 60 feet high and could take two or three years to carve.

The Coastal Indians used handmade tools for carving. The maul or hammer was made of stone with a wooden handle. The adz, which worked like an ax, was made with a sharpened flat, hard stone blade. And chisels for carving were made from sharpened stone or animal horn. After the totem poles were carved, they were sometimes painted with animal hair brushes. The paint colors were made from bark, coal, clay, copper, berries, and shells that were mixed with crushed salmon eggs. Black, red, blue, green, and white were the most common colors painted on totem poles.

When the pole was finished, it was ready to be raised and put into place. If the totem pole was to be used for a doorway, a large hole was cut through the bottom as the entrance. To set up the giant poles the Coastal Indians dug a hole in the ground and put the bottom of the pole into the hole. Then, with many men using ropes, they pulled the pole to an upright position.

Make Your Own Totem Pole

 Cut out or trace the figures and assemble your own totem.

The BEAVER was the symbol of patience, wisdom, healing, and wealth. He had two big front teeth and a cross-hatched tail.

The WHALE was the symbol of power, strength, and bravery. He had a dorsal fin on his back and a large mouth.

The THUNDERBIRD was the symbol of power in the sky. He controlled the thunder and lightning. He is usually at the top of the totem pole. His wings are always out-stretched. He was a messenger from the sky.

The BEAR was the symbol of power on the earth. He had a short snout, large teeth and was usually shown with his tongue sticking out.

The EAGLE was the symbol of wisdom and power. He warned and guarded the Indians. His curved beak points down toward the ground.

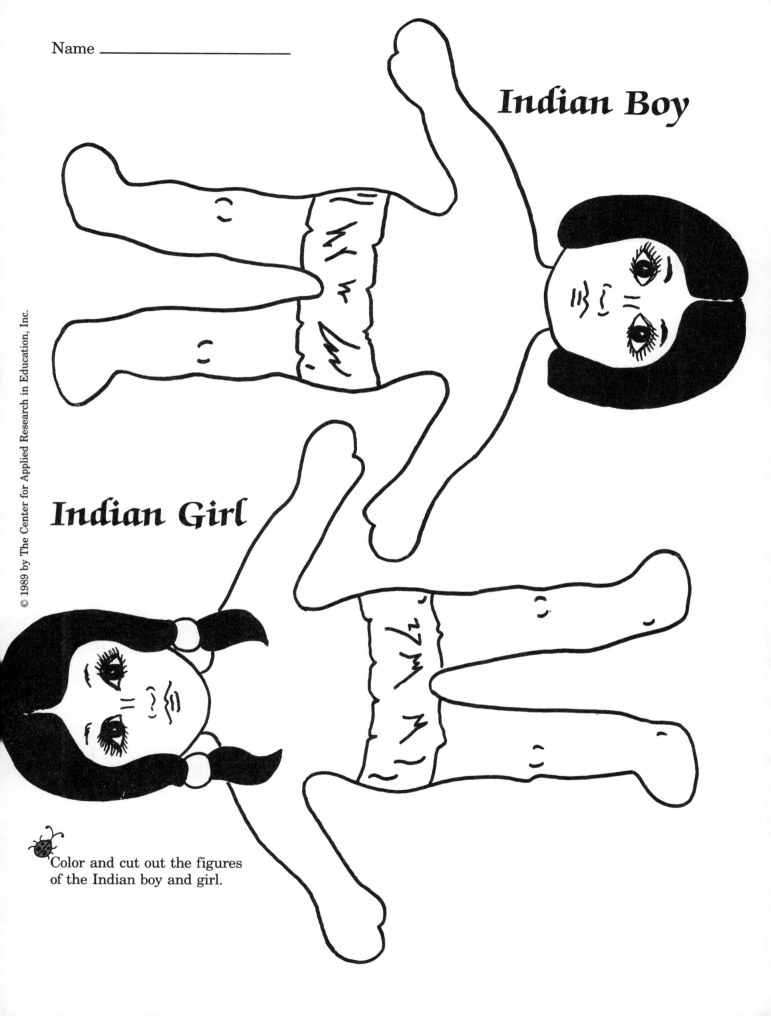

Name _____

Indian Boy

Indian Girl

Color and cut out the figures
of the Indian boy and girl.

Name _____

Woodland Boy

The Woodland Indian boy wears a breech-clout in the summer and buckskin leggings in the winter. Color his clothing tan. Cut around the clothing and tabs.

Woodland Girl

The Woodland Indian girl wears a tan buckskin dress decorated with beads and porcupine quills. Color and cut around the clothing and tabs.

Plains Boy

Color the Plains Indian boy's clothing tan. Cut around the outside of the clothing and tabs.

Plains Girl

Color the Plains Indian girl's animal hide clothing tan. Cut around the outside of the clothing and tabs.

Name _____

Desert Boy

Color the Desert Indian boy's woven poncho a bright color. The necklace and belt are turquoise and silver. Cut around the outside edges and tabs.

Desert Girl

Color the Desert Indian girl's top and skirt with several bright colors. The necklace is turquoise and silver. Cut around the outside edges and tabs.

Name _____

Coastal Boy

Color the Coastal Indian boy's cedar-bark clothing reddish brown. Cut around the outside edges and tabs.

Coastal Girl

Color the Coastal Indian girl's clothing reddish brown to look like cedarbark. Cut around the outside edges and tabs.

Name _____

Indian State Names

Thousands of places in the United States have names taken from Native American languages. Many cities, towns, mountains, and rivers are named for the people who first lived in the area.

Eight of the states in the United States got their names from Native American Tribes.

 Unscramble each group of letters to make the name of a state. Each state's name came from the name of a Native American Tribe.

What tribes originally lived near your home?

1. NASSAK _____

2. ROISMIUS _____

3. HUTA _____

4. SAANKSRA _____

5. SLINLIOI _____

6. WOAI _____

7. CHAMGINI _____

8. MABALAA _____

Name _____

Indians Quick Check

Use the word box to help you complete the sentences.

Woodland	Plains
Desert	Coastal

1. The _____ Indians lived along the western coast of the United States.

2. _____ Indians were dependent on the buffalo for their food and clothing.

3. Fine weaving, pottery, and jewelry were made by the _____ Indians.

4. Early explorers on the East Coast were met by the _____ Indians.

5. _____ Indians lived in hogans and pueblos.

6. The salmon was the main source of food for the _____ Indians.

7. The _____ Indians were nomadic hunters who traveled from place to place.

8. Sequoya, a _____ Indian, invented an alphabet.

Write "Yes" for true and "No" for not true.

9. ____ Corn was an important crop to the Coastal Indians.

10. ____ Woodland Indians made birchbark canoes.

11. ____ Sacajawea helped to lead the Lewis Clark Expedition.

12. ____ All American Indian groups spoke the same language.

13. ____ Coastal Indians were known for carving totem poles.

14. ____ Eight states in the United States got their names from Indian tribes.

15. ____ Kachinas were spirit figures worshiped by the Woodland Indians.

*BONUS: If you could be a member of one of the Indian groups that you have learned about, which one would you choose and why?

_____

_____

SECTION THREE

AMERICAN HERITAGE

Name _____

Explorers Word Search

Look for each of these explorers' names in the word search. The names can be found either across or down.

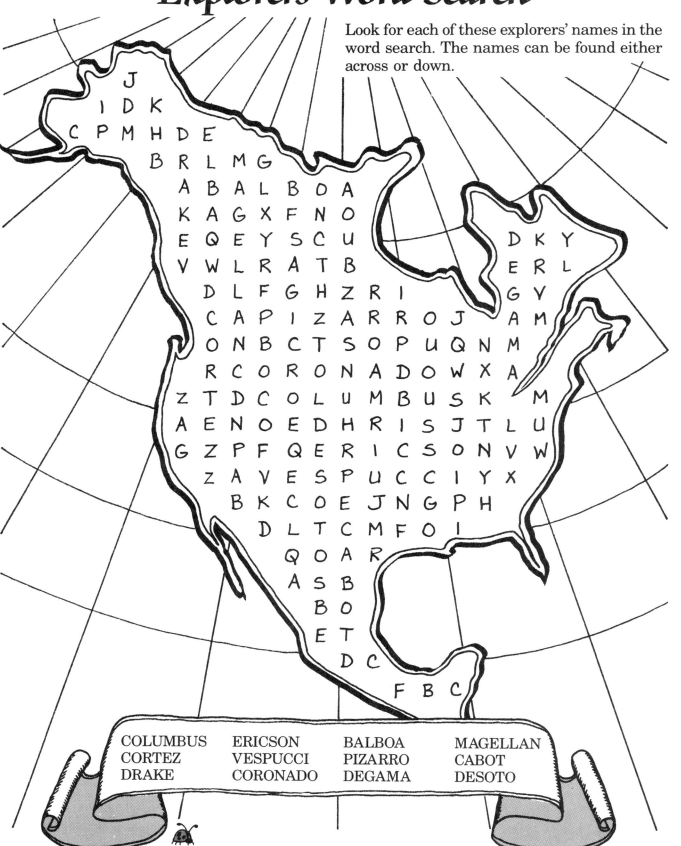

```
        J   D   K
      I   M   H   D   E
      C P     R   L   M G
          B     A   L   B   O   A
          A   A   G   X   F   N   O
          K   Q   E   Y   S   C   U
          E   V   W   L   R   A   T   B
          V   D   L   F   G   H   Z   R   I              D   K   Y
              C   A   P   I   Z   A   R   R   O   J    E   R   L
              O   N   B   C   T   S   O   P   U   Q N  G   V
              R   C   O   R   O   N   A   D   O   W X  A   M
          Z   T   D   C   O   L   U   M   B   U   S K A  M
          A   E   N   O   E   D   H   R   I   S   J T    U
          G   Z   P   F   Q   E   R   I   C   S   O N V  W
              Z   A   V   E   S   P   U   C   C   I   Y X
              B   K   C   O   E   J   N   G   P   H
              D   L   T   C   M   F   O   I
              Q   O   A   R
              A   S   B
              B   O
              E   T
              D   C
                    F   B   C
```

COLUMBUS	ERICSON	BALBOA	MAGELLAN
CORTEZ	VESPUCCI	PIZARRO	CABOT
DRAKE	CORONADO	DEGAMA	DESOTO

Name _____

Discovery Maze

On October 10, 1492, the crew of Columbus' first voyage decided to mutiny. After nine weeks of sailing west across the unknown sea, they were afraid. The very next morning, twigs were seen floating near the ships. Birds flew over the ships. The crew was convinced to give Columbus two more days to find land. At two o'clock in the morning of October twelfth the crew of the Pinta sighted land. America was discovered by moonlight!

Help the Pinta find her way across the sea. Draw a line from the ship to Watling Island.

All About Early Explorers

 ## Ready:

| merchant |
| European |
| route |
| spices |
| difficult |
| trade |
| voyage |
| material |
| circumnavigate |
| daring |
| colonies |
| explorers |

1. What word means to travel around the world by water?

   _____

2. _____ means a course or line of travel.

3. A journey made by water is a _____.

4. If you exchange goods, you_____them.

5. Seasonings used on food are _____.

6. Another name for a person who buys or sells goods is a

   _____.

 ## Set:

Over four hundred years ago, European merchants traveled east by land and sea to trade with merchants in Asia. These Europeans traded woolen goods, silver, tin, gold, and leather goods for spices, jewels, and silk material from Asia. The trade routes were very difficult, dangerous, and expensive to use. It could take many months, and sometimes even years for a box of spices to travel from Asia to Europe.

In the late 1400's people dreamed of discovering an all water route between Europe and Asia. Most explorers of the time believed the best route would be to travel around the tip of Africa and then eastward toward Asia.

But Christopher Columbus, knowing the world was round, began sailing westward. Instead of reaching Asia, Columbus landed on the coast of an unknown New World we call North America.

After Columbus died, a Spanish explorer named Balboa followed the western route and discovered the "great south sea" that we know as the Pacific Ocean.

In 1519 another Spanish explorer named Magellan began a journey that was of the greatest voyages in history. Sailing from Spain, he traveled around the tip of South America and across the Pacific Ocean. From the Philippine Islands, Magellan sailed around the tip of Africa and returned to Spain in 1522. Magellan did what no one else had ever done before—he circumnavigated the world!

In the years that followed the discovery of the New World, other daring men from Spain, Portugal, England, the Netherlands, and France began to explore and claim these lands for their own countries. As time passed, settlers came to the New World and established the first colonies in North America.

 Go:

1. About 440 years ago merchants traveled _____ to reach Asia.

2. What were the explorers looking for in the late 1400's? They were looking for an .

3. In which direction did Christopher Columbus sail? (North, West, East)

4. We now call the New World_____.

5. Balboa discovered the (Pacific, Atlantic, Indian) Ocean.

6. What word in paragraph five means to travel around the world by water?

_____

Explorers' Routes

On the next page you will find a map of the world. Read the instructions and complete the explorers' map.

Label these continents: North America, South America, Europe, Asia, Africa, Antarctica, and Australia. Color the continents green.

Label these oceans: Atlantic Ocean, Pacific Ocean, Arctic Ocean, and Indian Ocean. Color these water areas blue on your map.

The -------- lines on the map represent early trade routes on land and sea that were used to travel between Europe and Asia. Trace over the lines.

The _.__ lines on the map show how Christopher Columbus sailed westward to discover North America. Trace over the _.__ lines across the Atlantic Ocean to North America.

The _._._. lines on the map represent the exploration of Vasco de Balboa and his discovery of the Pacific Ocean. Trace over the _._._._ lines.

The .... lines on your map show the famous journey made by Ferdinand Magellan as he circumnavigated the world. Trace over the .... and follow his journey across the Atlantic Ocean, around South America, across the Pacific Ocean. Return to the right side of the map and continue to follow the .... across the Indian Ocean, around Africa, and back to Europe.

Roll your map into a cylinder so Magellan can circumnavigate the world.

Early Explorers   ------- Balboa
------- Columbus   ········· Magellan

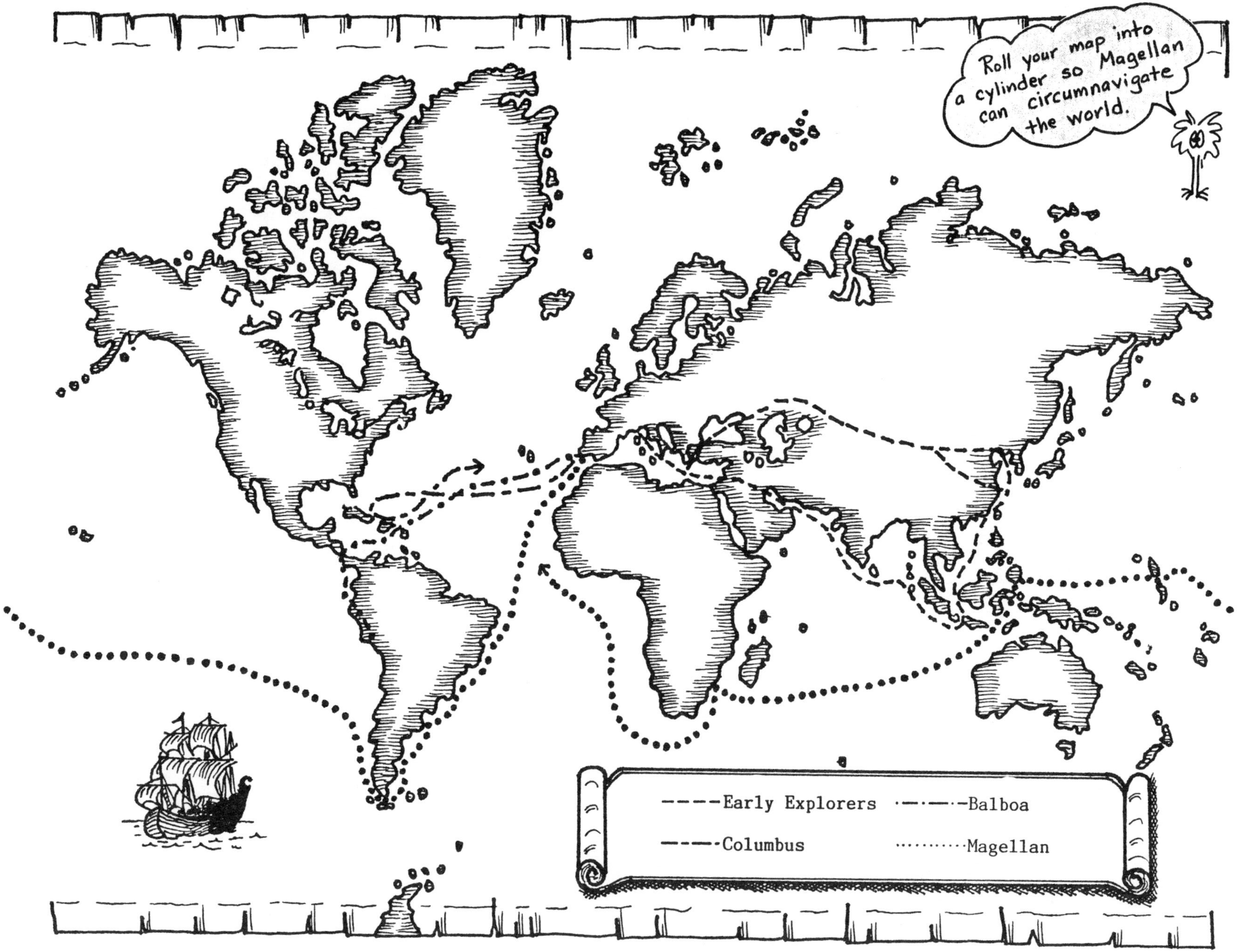

Name _____

Columbus Wasn't First

As you read this story, circle the correct word in each numbered box at the bottom of the sheet.

A thousand years ago the Vikings lived along the shores of northwestern Europe. They 1._____ the sea and were skillful sailors. The early Vikings sailed west from Norway and discovered Iceland. From there, other Viking 2._____ traveled farther west to the shores of Greenland.

The most famous Viking explorer was Leif Ericson. 3._____ 500 years before Christopher Columbus's voyage, Leif Ericson crossed the Atlantic Ocean from Greenland to Norway. On his return trip, Leif and his crew were 4._____ off course in the stormy seas. Finally, they made a safe landing on the northeast coast of what we know as 5._____ America. He named the country where he landed Vinland.

Leif Ericson left no maps that told of where he had 6._____ . In 1965 historians found an old 7._____ of the world that had been drawn in 1440. It showed Vinland to be part of North America. This map had been 8._____ at least 50 years 9._____ Columbus set sail for the New World. The map proved that Leif Ericson was one of the first men to 10._____ mainland America. The map also helps us to understand why Leif Ericson is often called "the discoverer of North America."

1. cared disliked loved	2. explorers soldiers children	3. near close almost	4. flew blown knocked	5. West North East
6. seen died sailed	7. table map graphs	8. construct delivered drawn	9. before near after	10. travel found visit

Name _____

All About the Aztecs

 Ready:

| solar |
| bartered |
| calendars |
| harvested |
| sacrifices |
| sacred |
| alphabet |
| vanished |
| warriors |
| waterways |

1. What word means about the same as "soldiers"? _____

2. Write the two small words in "waterways." _____ _____

3. What word has the same "h" sound as in the word "help"?

   _____

4. What objects measure days, weeks, months and years? _____

5. Another word for "disappeared" is_____

 Set:

Long before the Spanish explorers, the Aztec tribes came to the Valley of Mexico. They built their capital, Tenochtitlan, on an island in Lake Texcoco. By 1350 this city was bigger than any city in Europe.

The Aztec people were warriors, priests, craftsmen, merchants, farmers and slaves. They worshiped many gods.

Aztec farmers built floating gardens called "chinampas." These chinampas were joined to Tenochtitlan by waterways. The Aztec farmers always planted five seeds in each hole. Four corner seeds were for the gods of the four winds. The seed in the center was for the god of growth.

Farmers harvested their crops and brought their crafts to the city to trade. They had no money system, but bartered for goods they wanted. Cocoa beans were used for small change.

Few animals were raised for food by the Aztecs. They ate maize, beans, frogs, and fish. They raised rabbits, turkeys, and dogs. Chocolate and roasted puppy were favorite foods.

The Aztecs invented two calendars. Their solar calendar had 365 days just like ours. Their second calendar was sacred and had just 260 days in each year. They used both calendars at the same time!

Most of what we know about the Aztec people comes from their picture writing or "glyphs." Glyphs are like rebus pictures. The Aztecs had no alphabet, but they did have number symbols for counting.

The Spanish captured Tenochtitlan around 1520. Everything was destroyed and the city vanished. Hundreds of years later Lake Texcoco was drained and filled. Mexico City, the capital city of Mexico stands there today.

 Go:

1. The capital of the Aztec Empire was _____.

2. What did the Aztec farmers call their floating gardens? _____

3. The Aztecs had both coins and paper money. (Yes, No)

4. In paragraph seven, which word means "picture writing"?_____

5. The Aztec solar calendar had the same number of days as our present day calendar. (Yes, No)

6. Four seeds were planted to the gods of the four winds. What god was the fifth seed

   planted for?_____

7. The _____ captured and then destroyed the city of Tenochtitlan.

Name ______________________

Handwriting—Early Settlement

colony ______________________________

settlement ______________________________

voyage ______________________________

Mayflower ______________________________

Pilgrims ______________________________

expedition ______________________________

permanent ______________________________

hardships ______________________________

Jamestown ______________________________

New World ______________________________

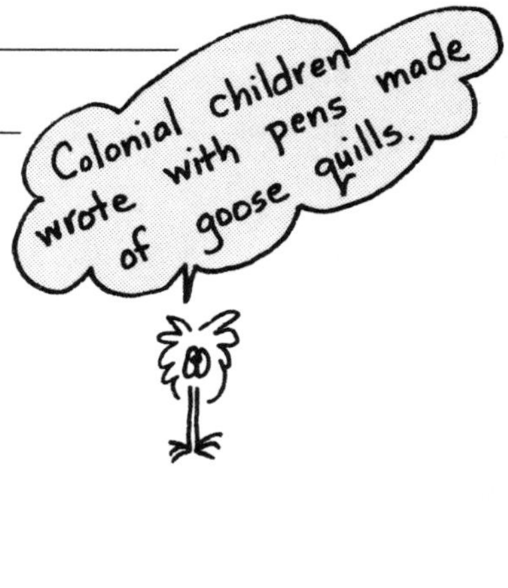
Colonial children wrote with pens made of goose quills.

Name _____

The Lost Colony

As you read this story, circle the correct word in each numbered box at the bottom of this sheet.

In 1587 a group of 121 men, women, and children arrived from England to establish a colony on Roanoke Island off the coast of what is now the state of North

Carolina. Once 1. _____ were settled, their Governor returned to England for supplies. England was at

war and the Governor was unable to 2. _____ to Roanoke Island for three years.

When the Governor did return in 1590, he found that all of the colonists had vanished! The only clues

3. _____ behind were the word "CROATOAN" carved into the bark of a 4. _____ near

the gate of the fort, and the letters "CRO" carved into a piece of bark found 5. _____ on the ground.

Some people believe the colonists moved to Croatan Island and were killed by the

Indians. Others 6. _____ the colonists were taken in by the Croatan Indians and

7. _____ of their tribe. Over 100 years later, hunters found a tribe of Indians with light

skin and blue eyes who 8. _____ English. These people had the same family names as

the colonists who had vanished. This group may have 9. _____ the descendants of the

colonists of Roanoke Island, but no one 10. _____ ever know for sure.

Roanoke comes from an Indian word meaning "shell money."

1.	2.	3.	4.	5.
we	return	lost	tree	floating
they	seek	near	house	lying
them	leave	left	trail	sitting
6.	7.	8.	9.	10.
know	members	talks	wanted	will
believe	tribes	reads	been	see
understand	groups	spoke	names	does

All About the First Colonies

 *Ready:*

struggle
permanent
founded
hardships
survivors
established
self-supporting
valuable
fashionable
severe

1. People who live through hardships are called _____.

2. What word comes from the root word "value"? _____

3. Two words that mean "began or started" are _____ and _____.

4. _____ means "long lasting."

5. A word that begins with the same sound as the word "strong" is _____.

6. Something very bad is _____.

 *Set:*

In the early 1600s people began to leave Europe to go to the New World. They settled along the east coast between what is now Virginia and Massachusetts. Settlers left Europe for many different reasons, but all had to struggle with the same problems.

Jamestown was the first permanent English settlement. The colony was founded in 1607. These Virginians were not prepared for hard times. The colonists faced many hardships including short food supplies, illness, and severe weather. The winter of 1609-1610 was the "starving time." Of the 500 colonists, 450 died. The survivors began to grow tobacco to send to Europe to support the colony.

Plymouth Colony was established by the Pilgrims. They arrived aboard the Mayflower in 1620. Many came to the New World because they wanted religious freedom. As in Jamestown, many in Plymouth became sick and died.

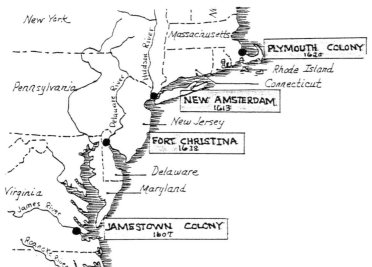

The colonists worked hard. They learned to fish, hunt and grow corn from the Indians and became self-supporting.

The Dutch came to the Hudson River area in 1613. In 1626 a group of thirty families settled in a colony called New Amsterdam. They brought cattle, horses, sheep, and pigs. They were well prepared for the hard life. The Dutch traded with the Indians for valuable beaver furs. The furs were sent to Europe and used for fashionable hats. Years later the English renamed New Amsterdam New York.

Fort Christina was settled by people from Sweden in 1638. They dreamed of the freedom to work, think, and worship as they pleased. The colonists bought land from the Indians, built a fort, and started a trading post. The Swedes were the first to build log cabins in America.

 Go:

1. Jamestown was founded by the (French, English, Dutch).

2. Religious freedom was one reason that people came to settle in the New World. (Yes, No)

3. _____ was the first Dutch colony in the Hudson River area.

4. _____ taught the Pilgrims of Plymouth to fish, hunt, and plant corn.

5. Survivors of Jamestown's "starving time" began to grow _____ to send to Europe.

6. The _____ built the first log cabins in America.

7. The Dutch trapped _____ to send to Europe for hats.

Some early settlers were lawbreakers who escaped punishment by coming to America.

Name _____

Colonial Schools

As you read this story, circle the correct word in each numbered box at the bottom of the page.

Soon after settling in America, the colonists started schools. At first children were taught in women's homes. These "dame schools" were much like preschools 1. _____ . In 1642 Massachusetts law said that all children should be taught to 2. _____ . Even so nine out of ten children never went to school!

Later one-room schoolhouses were built. These "grammar schools" were very 3. _____ from your school. There were no desks, pictures or chalkboards and usually only two or three books for the whole 4. _____ . Children sat on benches and had to bring firewood to heat the classroom. Teachers had no homes and took turns living with the student's families.

5. _____ were done on "hornbooks" which were not really books at all. They were pieces of 6. _____ on a wooden paddle. Often children made their own books by stitching 7. _____ sheets of paper. They made writing 8. _____ by boiling maple bark. Teachers sharpened goose quills for pens.

Colonial 9. _____ attended school about two months per year. Few children stayed in school more than two or three years. Boys went to school all day. Girls were 10. _____ for two hours in the late afternoon or between 5:00 and 7:00 in the morning!

1.	2.	3.	4.	5.
have	run	alike	school	Children
today	type	different	teacher	School
many	read	same	colony	Lessons
6.	7.	8.	9.	10.
plastic	together	pencil	soldiers	taught
ink	apart	ink	children	slept
paper	none	books	families	school

© 1989 by The Center for Applied Research in Education, Inc.

Linsey-Woolsey

Children in colonial times wore hand woven clothing made of a fabric called linsey-woolsey. Linsey-woolsey was a rough, scratchy cloth that was half linen and half wool. Linen was used for half of the cloth because the colonists did not have enough wool. Read the sentences in each column and number them from one to five to show how linsey-woolsey was made.

_____ The fleece was dyed and dried.

_____ The wool was spun into yarn for weaving.

_____ The sheep were sheared in the spring using hand clippers.

_____ The wool fleece was combed and carded to straighten out and blend the fibers.

_____ The sheared wool, called fleece, was washed to clean out dirt and oil.

_____ The flax was pulled from the ground in the late summer.

_____ The flax stalks were then combed and kept wet for two to three weeks to separate the woody bark and straw from the flax.

_____ Linen comes from the stalks of the flax plant.

_____ The flax was dried and combed again. Then it was spun into linen thread.

_____ The pulled stalks were tied into bundles and dried in the sun.

_6_ To make linsey-woolsey cloth, the linen thread was woven with the threads running up and down. The woolen threads were woven crosswise to form the filling of the cloth.

Linseed oil is made from pods from the flax plant.

Everyday Things

The four words listed below are not often used today. But, if you had lived in colonial times, these were the names of things that you might have used every day. Look up these words in the dictionary and write the definition below.

tallow _____

_____

wicks _____

_____

tinder _____

_____

trench (trencher) _____

_____

Next, look at the pictures below. Read about how each of these objects was used in colonial times. Use one of the words from the list above to complete each description.

Dry material that would ignite easily was

kept in a _____ box. To start a fire, they would strike a spark and light the contents of the box.

Wax for candles was made from melted

animal fat called _____ . It was poured into molds and allowed to cool and form the candle.

blade

Before lighting a candle, a special pair of unusual scissors were used to trim off the

burnt ends of the candle _____ so that they could be relighted.

The colonists had very few pottery dishes. Most everyday plates were carved or whittled from squares of wood. These plates

were called _____ .

Name _____

Now and Then

The settlers of long ago lived much differently than you live today. Read about how these people lived in the past. Then, write about how you live today to show how your life compares with the past.

Many people believe that the early colonists lived in log homes. This is not true. Their first homes were cottages like the homes that they had in Europe. These homes had thatched roofs made from reeds, straw, and grasses. There were plenty of trees in the colonies and soon they began to use these building materials to make plank houses with shingle roofs and stone fireplaces. The first log homes were built by the Swedish colonists in Delaware in about 1638.

_____
_____
_____
_____

During the first years the colonists were here in America, they had a difficult time providing food for their families. The Indians introduced them to corn and it became their basic food. Later, they began to raise their own vegetables and grains. In the fields and woodlands they hunted for meat, wild game, and berries. Fish and shellfish were caught in the rivers and ocean. The colonists did not have ways to preserve food, so most of their meals during the winter months were only bread and meat.

_____
_____
_____
_____
_____

The early colonists did not often travel far from their homes because the first roads were only narrow paths or Indian trails. The colonists had to travel by foot, on horseback or in carts or wagons pulled by horses or oxen. Later, after roads were widened and bridges were built, stagecoaches began to provide transportation from town to town.

_____

_____

_____

_____

_____

In the beginning, the colonists had very little chance to communicate with each other. Most communication and news was spread by word of mouth. They learned about the news from peddlers and travelers. Often these peddlers and travelers would carry letters with them from town to town. The first colonial mailmen were called postriders. They carried letters and messages on a route called a postroad. The town crier read the messages to people along the route. Later, newspapers were started to spread the news.

_____

_____

_____

_____

_____

If you could decide between living in colonial times and living now, which would you choose? Use the space below to explain your choice.

_____

_____

_____

Name _____

Heritage Handwriting

allegiance _____

_____

constitution _____

_____

freedom _____

_____

government _____

_____

independence _____

_____

liberty _____

_____

monument _____

_____

pledge _____

_____

republic _____

_____

union _____

_____

democracy _____

_____

Name _____

All About the Boston Tea Party

 **Ready:**

anchored
disguise
cargo
repeal
protest
remove
products
parliament
required
merchants

1. The goods carried by ship are called the ship's _____.

2. To complain about something is to _____.

3. _____ are storekeepers who sell goods.

4. You put on a _____ to hide the way you really look.

5. _____ and _____ are two words that mean "to get rid of something."

6. If you must do it, it is _____.

 **Set:**

In 1763 the British Government needed money. King George III told the British Parliament to raise money by taxing the colonies in America. Parliament passed the Stamp Act. This law required the colonists to buy tax stamps for newspapers, wills, and other business papers.

The colonists were very angry about the new law. They did not think the taxes were fair because they did not vote for the new law. In 1766 Parliament repealed the Stamp Act.

Next the British Parliament passed a law taxing paper, glass, lead, paint, and tea. The colonists also protested this new law. They refused to buy these products.

Finally, Parliament removed all the taxes except the tea tax.

Many colonists still thought the taxes were unfair, because they had no say in making the laws. They refused to buy tea. Many merchants refused to sell tea even to people who would buy it. Tea was left to rot in storerooms. In New York and Philadelphia the colonists wouldn't allow ships loaded with tea into their harbors.

In December of 1773, British ships loaded with tea were anchored in Boston Harbor. The colonists would not unload the cargo of tea. The British governor would not let the ships return to England with the tea.

On the night of December sixteenth fifty men disguised as Indians boarded the British ships. Quickly they broke open the cargo of tea and dumped it into Boston Harbor. More than three hundred chests of tea worth thousands of dollars were lost.

The Boston Tea Party told the British how the colonists felt about the tax of tea and about any laws they weren't allowed to vote on.

🐞 *Go:*

1. _____ was king of England in 1763.

2. The first law passed by Parliament to tax the colonists was called the _____ .

3. Colonists thought the new law was (weak, fine, unfair).

4. The British tried to tax paper, glass, lead, paint, and tea. (Yes, No)

5. The colonists were angry, but bought tea anyway. (Yes, No).

6. In December 1773, (50, 25, 12) men threw tea into Boston Harbor.

7. The colonists did not want to pay taxes that they didn't _____ for.

Hasty Pudding

Native Americans taught the first European settlers to grow "Indian corn." This corn became the colonists' most important food. Governor Bradford of Plymouth Colony called it "more precious than silver."

The settlers like fresh roasted corn, but this was a rare treat. Most corn was dried and ground into meal. Cornmeal could be used for bread, but the usual way to cook it was as Hasty Pudding.

"Hasty" means "quick," but hasty pudding certainly was not quick to make. Cornmeal was boiled for hours in water or milk to make a firm, thick pudding. Hasty pudding had to be stirred often during its hours of cooking so it didn't burn on the bottom.

Colonial families ate hasty pudding at least twice a day with milk, gravy or maple syrup. Sometimes they ate nothing else for months at a time!

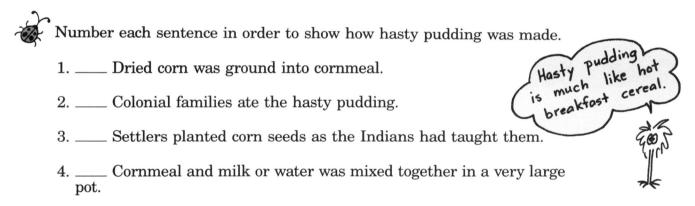

Number each sentence in order to show how hasty pudding was made.

1. _____ Dried corn was ground into cornmeal.

2. _____ Colonial families ate the hasty pudding.

3. _____ Settlers planted corn seeds as the Indians had taught them.

4. _____ Cornmeal and milk or water was mixed together in a very large pot.

5. _____ The corn was harvested and dried.

6. _____ The pudding was boiled and stirred for hours.

Hasty pudding is much like hot breakfast cereal.

What did Governor Bradford say about the corn the Indians taught the settlers of Plymouth Colony to plant?

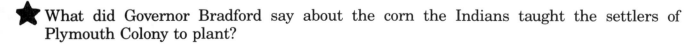

_____

_____

Name _____

Revolution

Fill in the date for each event. Cut them apart. Put the events in order. Paste them to a long strip of paper to make a timeline of the American Revolution.

THE STAMP ACT  date:_____	GEORGE WASHINGTON ELECTED PRESIDENT  date:_____

THE UNITED STATES CONSTITUTION  date:_____	PAUL REVERE'S RIDE  date:_____	THE BRITISH RECOGNIZE U.S. INDEPENDENCE  date:_____
THE BOSTON TEA PARTY  date:_____	THE ARTICLES OF CONFEDERATION  date:_____	THE DECLARATION OF INDEPENDENCE  date:_____

Name _____

All About the Constitution

 *Ready:*

convention
decade
framework
democracy
signature
ratify
principle
amendment
document
flexible

1. In a _____ everyone has a say in their government.

2. Ten years is a _____.

3. _____ means "can be changed."

4. The root word of _____ is "sign."

5. _____ is a compound word.

6. A special meeting is a _____.

 *Set:*

A decade after the Revolutionary War, fifty-five leaders of the thirteen states called a convention. They came together in Philadelphia, Pennsylvania, to create a new framework for the government of the United States of America. During the summer of 1787 they wrote and rewrote, argued and made speeches. In the fall thirty-nine men put their signatures on The Constitution of the United States of America.

In the 1780's there were just thirteen United States. Each one had to ratify or agree to the Constitution before it became the law of the land. Delaware was the first state to agree to the new Constitution in December of 1787. Rhode Island was the final state to ratify in May 1790.

The Constitution sets forth the principles or general rules that govern all United States citizens. It created a strong central government of representatives elected by the people. This form of government is called a democracy. Everyone has a say in how our country is run.

George Washington called the Constitution "the best that could be obtained at this time." The men who wrote it knew that it was not perfect. That is why they made the document flexible. They made it possible to change or add to the Constitution.

Changes in the Constitution are called amendments. The first ten amendments were all adopted at the same time in 1798. They are called "The Bill of Rights." The newest effort to change the Constitution is the Equal Rights Amendment. The Constitution has been amended only 25 times in more than two hundred years.

 Go:

1. The Constitutional Convention was called in the summer of _____ .

2. There were (55, 39, 13) men at the Constitutional Convention.

3. The Constitution created a strong central government. (Yes, No)

4. _____ was the first state to ratify the new Constitution.

5. Changes in the Constitution are called _____ .

6. The leaders who wrote the Constitution knew it (was, wasn't) perfect.

7. The Constitution has been the law of the land for over _____ years.

Name _____

Bill of Rights

As you read the story, circle the correct word in each numbered box at the bottom of this sheet.

The Bill of Rights was adopted by the U.S. on Dec. 15, 1791.

When it was first written, some people didn't agree with the new Constitution. There were many arguments about

1. _____ it should be adopted or not. Many of the people

against the 2. _____ thought that it did not protect individuals enough.

After the Constitution 3. _____ ratified, the first Congress proposed a bill of rights.

James Madison 4. _____ the original list. Thomas Jefferson supported the addition

5. _____ the Constitution. Jefferson feared that times would change and 6. _____ could forget their hard-fought freedoms.

The first ten amendments to the Constitution of the 7. _____ States Constitution

were adopted in 1791. These ten 8. _____ are the Bill of Rights. They guarantee us

freedom of speech, religion 9. _____ peaceful assembly. We are protected from cruel or unusual punishment. We have a right to privacy and to own property. The Bill of Rights

guarantees our 10. _____ of life, liberty, and the pursuit of happiness.

December 15th is "Bill of Rights Day."

1.	2.	3.	4.	5.
whether weather which	Declaration Speech Constitution	was were am	ate lost wrote	under from to
6.	7.	8.	9.	10.
people ratify propose	Divided United Rights	constitution congress amendments	and or but	rights first enough

Washington, D.C.

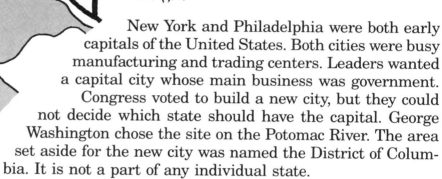

New York and Philadelphia were both early capitals of the United States. Both cities were busy manufacturing and trading centers. Leaders wanted a capital city whose main business was government. Congress voted to build a new city, but they could not decide which state should have the capital. George Washington chose the site on the Potomac River. The area set aside for the new city was named the District of Columbia. It is not a part of any individual state.

Washington, D.C. was carefully planned, but the building went slowly. George Washington did not live to see the first completed government building in the city named for him.

Use the map to help you answer these questions.

1. What street runs in front of the White House?

_____

2. What monument can be seen from both the Capitol and the White House?

_____

3. What street is the northern boundary of The Mall?

_____

4. What important building is across the Potomac from the White House?

_____

Name _____

George Washington

 Add to find the year that George Washington died. The first one is done for you.

Add Here

$$
\begin{array}{r}
1732 \\
+\ 19 \\
\hline
1751 \\
\end{array}
$$

George was born in 1732.

Nineteen years later George was a surveyor.

One year later, when his brother Lawrence died, George began his military career.

$+$ _____

George took part in a military campaign in Pennsylvania two years later.

$+$ _____

Five years later George married Martha Custia.

$+$ _____

George remained in retirement at his home, Mount Vernon, for sixteen years.

$+$ _____

George spent eight years as Commander-in-Chief of the Continental Army.

$+$ _____

Six years later George Washington was elected President of the United States of America.

$+$ _____

Washington was President for eight years.

$+$ _____

Two years after he left office, George Washington died at his home in Virginia.

$+$ _____

 ★ How many years did George Washington live?

★ _____

Citizenship Word Search

Look for each of these words in the word search. The words can be found either across or down.

Name _____

Where was the Constitution signed?

On the bottom!

```
      U N I O N
J H I W X R T P Q
K F E V U S K Y F B
A L L E G I A N C E A D
G C I U V F G R D E S Z
C O B I B E R T E R A Y A
X N E N H D L Q M A N B C
V S R D T E S O O N P J P
U T T E I R L T C T R J Q
W I Y P U A U J R H E K Q
K T S E M L G W A E A M X J
L U Y N M V K O C M M O H I
T M D Z F P X Y I B N Y D F
I C E N E R P Q W L U A B E
O N N P L E D G E E M X L C G H
N T C G O V E R N M E N T M Y N T
J R E P U B L I C H N R S A C I
B N M C D L Q O Z F T D G B
A H I S T O R I C A L E
F R E E D O M O
B P Z A
```

allegiance
federal
government
constitution
liberty

independence
monument
republic
pledge
union

anthem
democracy
freedom
historical
preamble

Name _____

Our National Anthem

As you read this story, circle the correct word in each numbered box at the bottom of this sheet.

"Oh, say can you see, by the dawn's early light,
What so proudly we hailed at the twilight's last gleaming?
Whose broad stripes and bright stars through the perilous fight,
O'er the ramparts we watched, were so gallantly streaming.
And the rockets' red glare, the bombs bursting in air.
Gave proof through the night that our flag was still there.
Oh, say does that Star-Spangled Banner yet wave,
O'er the land of the free and the home of the brave?"

Everyone has probably sung "The Star-Spangled Banner" many times. 1. _____ people understand its meaning 2. _____ they know its history. The National Anthem was 3. _____ during the War of 1812. The British had attacked Fort McHenry 4. _____ Baltimore. Francis Scott Key, an American, was watching the 5. _____ .

The British bombarded the fort all through the night. Key worried whether the 6. _____ could withstand the attack. Before dawn he 7. _____ writing. At eight o'clock in the morning the bombing stopped. The smoke 8. _____ the battle cleared away and Francis Scott Key could see the American flag still flying 9. _____ the fort. The words of his song still 10. _____ the story.

© 1989 by The Center for Applied Research in Education, Inc.

1.	2.	3.	4.	5.
Few	when	lost	under	battle
Two	until	sung	near	show
Many	if	written	over	rain
6.	7.	8.	9.	10.
forest	began	to	shipped	tell
soldiers	did	by	below	aren't
British	left	from	above	like

All About the Statute of Liberty

 Ready:

represents
monument
symbol
figure
torch
shackle
frame
spiral
core
pedestal
masses
teeming

1. The base of which something stands is called the _____.

2. What word rhymes with "came"?_____

3. The word that has the same sound as "or" or "door" is ____.

4. _____ is the base word found in "teeming."

5. Something built as a remembrance is called a _____.

6. _____ starts with the same sound as "shoe."

For her 200th birthday the Statue of Liberty got a "face lift."

 Set:

The Statue of Liberty represents freedom to people coming to America from many lands. France gave this monument to the United States in 1884 as a symbol of friendship between our two countries. Our country recently had a celebration for the 200th birthday of the Statue of Liberty.

The statue stands on Liberty Island in New York Harbor. The figure is a proud woman. She holds a burning torch in her right hand. On it is the date of the Declaration of Independence, July 4, 1776. At her feet is a broken shackle. This broken shackle represents the people winning their freedom.

The Statue of Liberty is 151 feet tall. Her index finger is 8 feet long. The statue's frame is made of metal. Over this metal frame sheets of copper were carefully hammered. This gives the outside of the statue a copper finish.

A visitor may climb to the crown of the statue's head. Two spiral staircases go up through the core of the statue. Another stairway inside the right arm leads to the torch.

On the pedestal of the Statue of Liberty is a poem. The poem is called "The New Colossus" by Emma Lazarus. You may have heard these famous lines from her poem:

"Give me your tired,
    your poor, your huddled massed,
Yearning to breathe free,
    the wretched refuse of your teeming shore.
Send these, the homeless,
    tempest-tossed to me,
I lift my lamp
    beside the golden door."

 Go:

1. The Statute of Liberty was given to the United States by (Spain, England, France).

2. The United States received the statue in (1776, 1884, 1984).

3. The statue is 151 feet tall. (Yes, No)

4. What kind of finish does the statue have? _____

5. What word from paragraph 4 means the same thing as "winding"? _____

6. The Statue of Liberty is in Boston. (Yes, No)

7. At the feet of the statue is a broken (jar, shackle, crown).

All About "The Pledge of Allegiance"

 Ready:

recite
final
separate
indivisible
individual
representative
devotion
loyalty
solemn
pledge
allegiance
meaning

1. What word rhymes with "light"? _____

2. A word that means "serious and important" is _____ .

3. _____ begins with the same sound as the word "play."

4. If you can't split something apart it is _____ .

5. _____ means "the last one."

6. A word with the same "tion" sound

   you hear in "nation" is _____ .

Set:

"I pledge allegiance to the flag
of the United States of America
and to the Republic for which it stands,
one Nation, under God, indivisible,
with liberty and justice for all."

These words were written by Francis Bellamy of Boston in 1892. Every school child in our country learns "The Pledge of Allegiance," but few people really understand its full meaning.

When you pledge your allegiance you make a solemn promise. You promise your loyalty and devotion to your nation and its people.

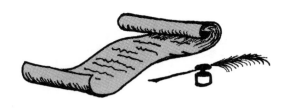

"The Pledge of Allegiance" includes the words "one Nation." Our country is made up of fifty individual states. Even though each state is different from all of the others, they make a single country. "Indivisible" means that our country can never be divided. No state or group of states can separate from the others.

The final words of the "Pledge of Allegiance" are "with liberty and justice for all." This is the great goal of Americans to make laws that are fair to everyone. Our nation is a "republic." This is the type of government where leaders are elected by all the people. These representatives speak for those who elect them. Under our form of government all people should be free and equal.

Next time you recite the "Pledge of Allegiance" listen carefully and remember your promise.

🐞 Go:

1. A person elected to speak for others is a (republic, representative, speaker).

2. Our country is made up of (13, 48, 50) states.

3. "Allegiance" means _____ and _____.

4. Francis Bellamy wrote "The Pledge of Allegiance" in 1792. (Yes, No)

5. Our nation is a republic. (Yes, No)

6. What word from paragraph 4 means "cannot be divided"?_____

7. The great goal of Americans is "liberty and _____ for all."

Name _____

Important Events

Read about these important events in the history of our country.
Then follow the directions at the bottom of the page.

★ **Columbus** first sighted America on October 12, *1492*. He opened the New World to European exploration.

★ **Jamestown,** Virginia, was the first permanent English settlement in America. It was founded in *1607* by the London Company.

★ **The Pilgrims** settled in America for religious reasons. They landed in Plymouth, Massachusetts, in *1620*.

★ **Paul Revere** rode to warn the colonists about the British troops. This event in *1775* marked the beginning of the Revolution.

★ **The Constitution** is the set of laws by which the United States is governed. It was written in *1787*.

★ **George Washington** was our first President. Few people know that he did not begin his term until *1789*.

★ **The Star Spangled Banner** was written in *1814* by Francis Scott Key during the battle at Fort McHenry.

★ **The Statue of Liberty** represents freedom and liberty. In *1884* it was given to the U.S. by France.

★ **The Pledge of Allegiance** was written in *1892* by Francis Bellamy of Boston.

1. On the next page, find a picture that goes with each event. Fill in the date on the line.

2. Cut out the pictures along the dark lines.

3. Place the pictures in the order the events happened.

4. Glue the pictures on a strip of paper to make a timeline.

Our National Anthem

date: _____

Statue of Liberty

date: _____

Jamestown

date: _____

Paul Revere

date: _____

The Pilgrims

date: _____

The Constitution

date: _____

Pledge of Allegiance

date: _____

George Washington

date: _____

Columbus

date: _____

Citizenship Crossword

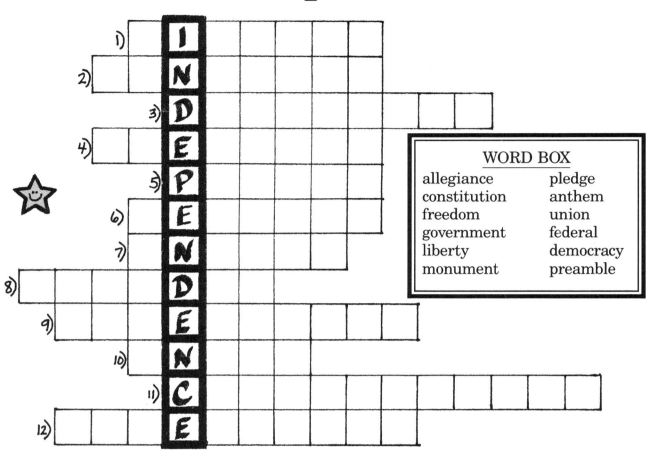

WORD BOX

allegiance	pledge
constitution	anthem
freedom	union
government	federal
liberty	democracy
monument	preamble

1. "…with _____ and justice for all."

2. something built as a remembrance of a person or event

3. rule by a government of, by, and for the people

4. an introduction

5. solemn promise

6. having to do with the central government of the United States

7. song of praise or devotion

8. without restraint or restriction

9. "I pledge _____ to the flag…"

10. group of people or states formed for a common good

11. set of laws governing a country

12. system to run a country or state

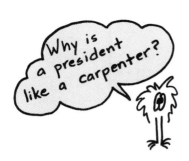

Government Handwriting

amendment _____

bill _____

Congress _____

cabinet _____

initiative _____

President _____

referendum _____

representative _____

Senate _____

Supreme Court _____
_____

Name _____

Look for each of these words in the word search. They can be found either across or down.

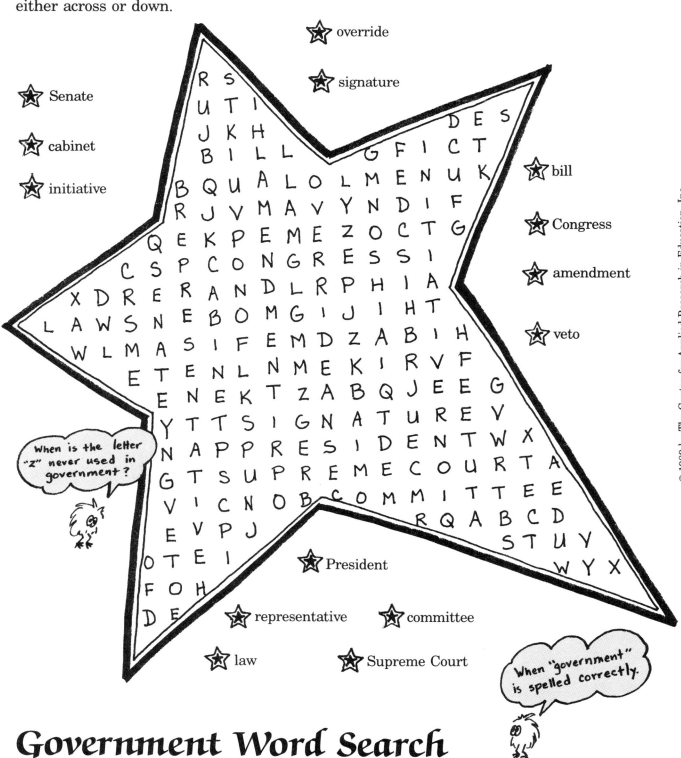

override

signature

Senate

cabinet

initiative

bill

Congress

amendment

veto

President

representative   committee

law   Supreme Court

When is the letter "z" never used in government?

When "government" is spelled correctly.

Government Word Search

Name _____

Three Branches

The Constitution is the plan for our government. We have a federal system of government. That means that our national government shares power with the fifty individual states. Our government is also a representative democracy. This means that the people choose their representatives by free ballot. Anyone may be elected and everyone can vote.

The leaders who wrote our Constitution wanted a government where no one had too much power. Our government has three branches or parts to divide the power of running our country. The three branches are the legislative branch, the executive branch, and the judicial branch.

The Congress is the legislative branch of our national government. The job of the legislative branch is to make our laws. Congress has two parts, the Senate and the House of Representatives. Every state has two Senators. The number of representatives is different for different states. States with many people have more representatives than states with few people. Every state has at least one representative in the House of Representatives.

The job of the executive branch of our government is to carry out the laws. The head of the executive branch is the President. He has many people to help him including the Vice President. He has a group of advisors called the Cabinet. The President appoints these advisors to be the heads of the many government departments. The cabinet helps the President make decisions.

The Supreme Court is the highest level of the Judicial branch of our government. There are nine justices or judges on the Supreme Court. Their job is to settle questions about the laws. The judicial branch is made up of other courts, too. Some are local and state courts.

Name _____

Each of the three branches of our government has some powers that affect the other two branches. This is called the system of checks and balances. This way no one branch becomes too powerful. The people always keep the power to govern themselves.

Define these words. Use the article to help you.

1. Democracy_____

_____

2. Representative_____

_____

3. Constitution_____

_____

Draw lines to match each to its branch and main job.

4.   SUPREME ★   ★ EXECUTIVE ★   ★ CARRIES OUT
         COURT   BRANCH   THE LAWS

5.   CONGRESS ★   ★ JUDICIAL ★   ★ MAKES THE
                           BRANCH   LAWS

6.   THE ★   ★ LEGISLATIVE ★   ★ SETTLES
       PRESIDENT   BRANCH   QUESTIONS

7. How many Senators does your state have?_____

8. How many Representatives does your state have?_____

Name _____

Congress

The legislative branch of our government is Congress. It is the job of the Congress to make our laws. The Congress has two parts or houses, the Senate and the House of Representatives. Members of both houses are elected directly by a vote of the people.

When our nation was young, some leaders were worried about the government becoming too powerful. They wanted the people to control their lawmakers. These leaders wanted direct election of the legislature. Some leaders wanted every state to have equal voting power. Others thought that large states should have more say than small states. In the end, they compromised and settled on the two-house congress.

The Senate is the Upper House of Congress. Senators are elected for six years. There are 100 Senators. Each state elects two Senators, so each state has an equal say in the Senate.

The House of Representatives is the Lower House. Representatives are elected every two years. There are 435 Representatives in the House of Representatives. The number of Representatives for each state depends on how many people live in that state. Some states have 25 or more Representatives. Every state has at least one Representative.

 Write "YES" if a statement is true. Write "NO" if a statement is not true.

1. ____ The Congress of the United States has two houses.

2. ____ Members of Congress serve four-year terms of office.

3. ____ Every state has two Representatives in the House of Representatives.

4. ____ There are 435 Senators in the United States Senate.

5. ____ Some states have more Representatives in the House of Representatives than other states.

How many Representatives does your state have?

6. ____ The main job of the United States Congress is to make our laws.

7. ____ Voters elect their Senators and Representatives by direct vote.

Name _____

All About Presidents

 *Ready:*

| executive |
| tailor |
| responsibility |
| interest |
| famous |
| limited |
| mediocre |
| powerful |
| appointed |
| nation |

1. Strong and _____ mean about the same thing.

2. "…one _____ under God, indivisible, with liberty and justice for all."

3. A _____ sews clothing.

4. The three branches of government are legislative, _____ and judicial.

5. The opposite of "endless" is _____.

6. Someone who is well-known is _____.

 *Set:*

The President of the United States is the head of the executive branch of our government. It is the job of the President to see that our laws are carried out.

Our President is different from the leaders of every other nation. Our President is very powerful, but that is not the difference. The difference is that our President holds power only for a limited time. We can change presidents every four years. No President may serve more than 10 years.

History records our Presidents' great events. Some things about our leaders are not so well known. Like you they had many different interests. John Quincy Adams was a poet.

Andrew Johnson was a skilled tailor and enjoyed making his own suits. Theodore Roosevelt ran laps around the Washington Monument for exercise. Dwight Eisenhower practiced golf on the lawn of the White House. John Kennedy enjoyed swimming and used the White House pool twice a day.

Some Presidents are remembered for things they did first. John Adams was the first President to live in the White House. Franklin Roosevelt was the first and only President to serve more than two terms. He also appointed the first woman to the Cabinet. Benjamin Harrison was the first President to have electricity in the White House.

Rutherford B. Hayes was called "one of the most mediocre-looking men ever to run for President." William Harrison had 48 grandchildren. One of them was Benjamin Harrison, our 23rd President.

Our nation has been lead by more than forty different Presidents. Some like Washington and Lincoln we remember for their great work. Some Presidents are not so famous, but all shared the responsibility of shaping our history and our country.

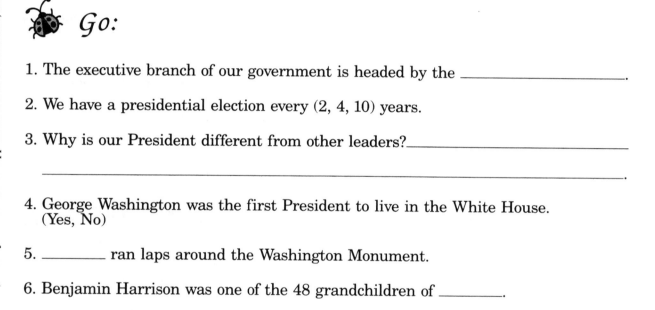 *Go:*

1. The executive branch of our government is headed by the _____.

2. We have a presidential election every (2, 4, 10) years.

3. Why is our President different from other leaders?_____

_____.

4. George Washington was the first President to live in the White House.
   (Yes, No)

5. _____ ran laps around the Washington Monument.

6. Benjamin Harrison was one of the 48 grandchildren of _____.

7. More than (40, 70, 100) Presidents have shared the responsibility of shaping our history and our country.

Name _____

The Supreme Court

As you read this story, circle the correct word in each numbered box at the bottom of this sheet.

The Supreme Court of the United States heads the judicial branch of our government. The main job of the Supreme 1. _____ is to settle questions about the law. It is the Supreme Court which decides 2. _____ laws agree with our Constitution.

There are nine justices or judges on the Supreme Court. If a new 3. _____ is needed the President appoints or chooses one. If the Senate agrees, that 4. _____ becomes a new 5. _____ Court Justice. Justices serve on the court for life. They can not be "fired" from 6. _____ jobs. This is so that Supreme Court justices can not be forced to 7. _____ decisions they don't really agree with.

The justices 8. _____ which cases they will hear or consider. Cases that are important to the most people are usually chosen. After listening 9. _____ studying both sides of the case carefully the Court rules. All the other courts in our 10. _____ must go by what the Supreme Court decides. Our Constitution says that everyone is created equal. Everyone in our country lives by the same laws. Above the entrance to the Supreme Court Building in Washington, D.C., are these words, "Equal Justice Under Law."

Sandra Day O'Connor joined the Court in 1981, as the 1st woman justice.

1.	2.	3.	4.	5.
Court	or	justice	court	United
State	if	president	law	Senate
Law	but	senator	person	Supreme
6.	7.	8.	9.	10.
its	make	forces	but	building
them	serve	decide	and	country
their	began	fooses	not	question

Name _____

Your Representatives

The United States government is a representative democracy. That means that people vote to decide who shall speak for them in their government. The people elected from your area represent YOU. This is so even if you are too young to vote yet. It is important to know as much as possible about the people who represent you.

Find out who has been elected to run YOUR government. Then answer the questions below.

1. Who is the President of the United States?

_____

2. Who is the Vice President of the United States?

_____

3. Who are your United States Senators? (each state has two)

_____

_____

4. What U.S. Congressional District do you live in?

_____

5. Who is your Representative in the U.S. House of Representatives?

_____

6. Who is Governor of your state?

_____

7. Who represents you in your state legislature?

_____

_____

In what year will you first be able to vote?

U.S. Coins

The first United States coins were minted in Philadelphia in 1793. Cents and half-cents were the first U.S. coins. At one time the U.S. used two-cent and three-cent coins. Today only the penny, nickel, dime, quarter and half-dollar are common.

 Use what you know about the value of coins to find the value of each row of coins.

1. QUARTER QUARTER DIME PENNY PENNY PENNY   _____ ¢

2. QUARTER DIME DIME DIME DIME PENNY   _____ ¢

3. DIME DIME NICKEL NICKEL PENNY PENNY   _____ ¢

4. QUARTER QUARTER QUARTER NICKEL NICKEL NICKEL   _____ ¢

5. DIME DIME NICKEL NICKEL NICKEL PENNY   _____ ¢

Name _____

Elections Handwriting

I vote for good handwriting

ballot _____

citizen _____

convention _____

campaign _____

candidate _____

election _____

inauguration _____

office _____

party _____

registration _____

Name _____

Voting!

"Ballot" comes from the French word "ballotte" meaning "little ball".

As you read this story, circle the correct word in each numbered box at the bottom of this sheet.

The Greeks were the first known voters about 2500 years ago. These ancient 1. _____ voted by dropping a certain colored ball into a pot. There are many 2. _____ kinds of voting—show of hands, roll call, voice vote. In the United 3. _____ we use a voting system called an "Australian ballot." An Australian 4. _____ is special because it is secret. No one can tell how you voted.

Before the election, voters 5. _____ the candidates and decide how they want to vote. On 6. _____ day each voter goes to their polling place. A 7. _____ place is usually a school, fire station or other public building. At the polling place each voter signs the register and is given a 8. _____. Voters mark their ballots. The ballots are folded and placed in a locked ballot box. In some places voting machines are used 9. _____ of paper ballots.

Voting goes on all day so that everyone can have a chance to 10. _____. After the polls closed the election clerks count the ballots. People are anxious to know who has won the election. As soon as the votes are counted, election officials give the results to the newspaper, television, and radio reporters. Soon everyone knows what the ballots said.

Ask your mom or dad if you can go along and watch next time they vote.

1.	2.	3.	4.	5.
Greece Greeks Poles	other under same	States Kingdom Nation	city state ballot	hide win study
6.	7.	8.	9.	10.
spring special election	polling decide system	voice dolor ballot	instead but like	vote use school

Name _____

Voter Registration

In the early days of the United States only wealthy white men could vote. Today nearly all adult U.S. citizens have the right and duty to vote in free elections.

In order to vote you must be eighteen years old. You must also register. This means that you must have your name listed with other voters on the county voting register. Registering voters make sure that they vote only where they live. It also keeps them from voting twice!

Fill in the Voter's Registration with your own information. You will be ready for the real thing when you are eighteen.

Women couldn't vote until 1920.

Native Americans couldn't vote until 1948!

OFFICIAL REGISTER OF VOTER

FIRST NAME	INITIAL	LAST NAME
RESIDENCE ADDRESS		
CITY OR TOWN		ZIP CODE
MALE FEMALE	DATE OF BIRTH	
HOME PHONE	SOCIAL SECURITY NUMBER	
STATE _____	COUNTY _____	

"I, the undersigned, on oath or affirmation, do hereby declare that the facts set forth herein relating to my qualifications as a voter, recorded by the registration officer in my presence, are true. I further certify that I am not presently denied my civil rights as a result of being convicted of an infamous crime and that I will be at least eighteen years of age at the time of voting."

SIGNATURE OF VOTER _____ DATE _____

PRINT NAME HERE FOR POSITIVE IDENTIFICATION

A Presidential Election

Elections take place every day in the United States and other democratic countries. You and your friends may vote which game to play. Juries vote to make decisions. The captains of sports teams are chosen by election.

One important kind of election decides who should hold public office. The people elected in these elections run our government. By law, the United States holds a general election every two years.

A Presidential election is held every four years in the U.S., but a Presidential election starts long before election day. First a candidate must declare she or he is a candidate for office. Most often the person makes a speech, sometimes on television or radio. Campaign workers also tell newspapers and magazines and the campaign has begun.

The first chance the public has to vote is in a Primary Election. Primaries are held because often many people want to run for President. A Primary narrows the choice of candidates. Only the candidates with the most votes will be in the General Election. Some states have a Caucus system instead of a Primary.

After the Primaries the major political parties have conventions. Delegates from every state meet to nominate their party's candidate. The nominated candidate will be in the General Election.

The candidates campaign right up to election day. They make speeches, hold meetings, shake hands, and talk with as many voters as possible. They try to visit every state in a few short months. Their supporters are also busy asking people to vote for their candidate.

On election day every registered voter may go to the polls and vote. Most public offices and issues are decided by direct vote. That means that people vote directly for their choice. Presidential elections are more complicated. We elect our President and Vice President indirectly. That means that voters don't actually vote for their favorite candidate. People vote for "electors." These electors actually elect the new leaders. After the General Election the electors cast their votes and directly elect the President and Vice President. This system of indirect election is called the Electoral College.

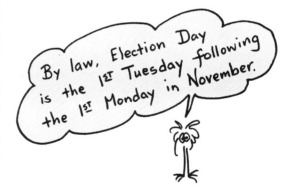

By law, Election Day is the 1st Tuesday following the 1st Monday in November.

Finally in January the new President and Vice President take office. They take the oath of office and are inaugurated as our new leaders.

Cut out the rectangles below. Lay them out, in order, to show the steps in a Presidential Election. Paste to another piece of paper. Title your paper "A PRESIDENTIAL ELECTION."

Electoral ★ ★ College

Candidate ★ ★ ★ Declares

VOTE FOR President!

General ★ ★ Election

NOVEMBER 3 TUESDAY

Primary ★ Elections

BALLOT

Inauguration ★ Day ★

★ Party Conventions ★

★ ★ ★ ★ ★ ★

All About Political Parties

 Ready:

democracy nominate candidate campaign major existence slavery minor convention delegation

1. Something _____ is large and important.

2. Something small and less importatn is called _____.

3. _____ and _____ are four-syllable words.

4. A _____ is a person who is running for public office.

5. A meeting of a large group of people is a _____.

6. Political parties select or _____ their choice of candidates.

 Set:

In a democracy, many people must work together for their candidate to win an election. A political party is a group of people who work together. They share the same ideas about who should be elected and about how the government ought to run.

Political parties are very important in a democracy like the United States. Political parties nominate candidates for public office. They raise money and campaign for their candidates.

Political parties also help balance power. Each party watches what the other is doing. If one party makes a mistake, the other is sure to let everyone know.

In the United States there are two major political parties, the Republicans and the Democrats. The Democratic Party has been in existence since our country was new. The donkey is the symbol of the Democratic Party. The present Republican Party grew from a group against slavery. Abraham Lincoln was the first Republican President. The elephant is the symbol of the Republican Party.

There are many minor political parties. No minor party has ever won the presidency, but they are still important. Often a minor party has brought attention to an issue. When enough people became interested the major parties help to solve these problems.

Every four years political parties have conventions. Representatives or delegates from each state gather to nominate candidates for President and Vice President of the United States. There is much excitement at a political convention. Bands play, people cheer, and there are signs and banners everywhere. Often parts of political party conventions are shown on television. Each state delegation has a sign with their state's name. If you get to see a convention, look for the delegation from your state.

 *Go:*

1. A _____ is a state representative to a political convention.

2. The two major political parties in the United States are the _____ Party and the

   _____ Party.

3. _____ was the first Republican President.

4. Minor parties are unimportant in the United States. (Yes, No)

5. Political parties hold conventions every (2, 3, 4) years.

6. We elect our leaders because the United States is a (candidate, campaign, democracy).

7. What is the symbol of the Democratic Party?_____

Name _____

The Election's End

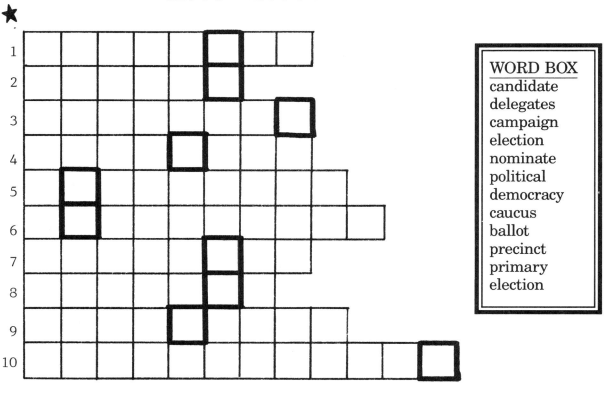

WORD BOX
candidate
delegates
campaign
election
nominate
political
democracy
caucus
ballot
precinct
primary
election

CLUES:

1. In a democracy an _____ is held to decide who leads the country.

2. A voter marks a _____ to show his or her choice for President.

3. A good _____ helps voters to know what a candidate stands for.

4. Voters must register and vote in their own _____ .

5. A _____ is someone running for a public office.

6. At a political party _____ candidates are nominated to run for office.

7. Political parties select or _____ candidates for public office.

8. Before the general election, _____ elections narrow the list of candidates.

9. Representatives or _____ of each state attend conventions.

10. Voters' _____ keeps people from voting twice.

BONUS CLUE: The Election's End

4.	3.	5.	u	9.	u	8.	7.	2.	1.	6.	10.

Name _____

Heritage Quick Check

 Use the word box to help you complete the sentences.

Hornbooks	lindsey-woolsey	Asia	Columbus
hardships	Magellan	hasty pudding	America
	tinderbox	tallow	

1. The Nina, Pinta, and Santa Maria were the ships of _____.

2. Early explorers were searching for a faster route to _____.

3. Early settlers in America had to overcome many_____.

4. _____ were made from pieces of paper attached to a wooden paddle.

5. A scratchy cloth called _____ was made from wool and linen.

6. Fires were started by using a _____.

7. Sometimes colonists ate nothing but _____ for months.

 Write "Yes" for true and "No" for not true.

8. ____ "Indivisible" means "can not be divided."

9. ____ The United States government has four branches.

10. ____ The Senate and the House of Representatives are the two houses of the United States Congress.

11. ____ Every state has two Senators and at least one Representative.

12. ____ The United States holds a presidential election every four years.

13. ____ A voter must vote in his or her own precinct.

14. ____ The Electoral College has a football team.

15. ____ Political parties are not very important in the United States.

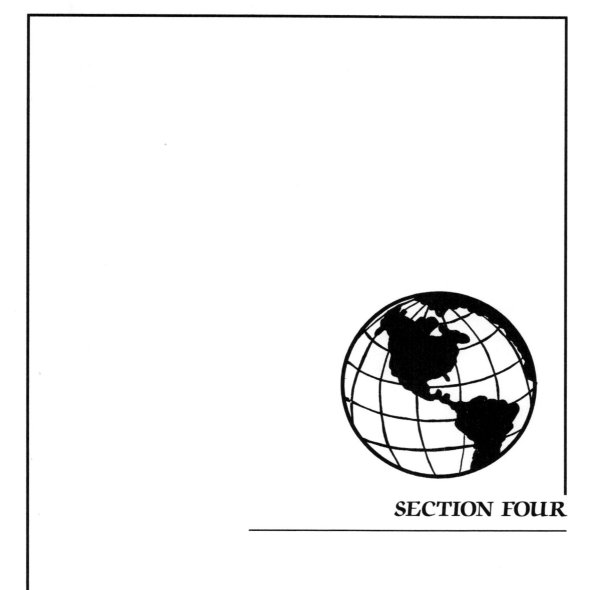

SECTION FOUR

WORLD REGIONS

Continents & Oceans Handwriting

North America _____

South America _____

Europe _____

Africa _____

Asia _____

Australia _____

Antarctica _____

Pacific Ocean _____

Atlantic Ocean _____

Indian Ocean _____

Arctic Ocean _____

Mixed-up Continents

DIRECTIONS:

1. Try to identify each of the seven continents by its shape.

2. Color the continents green. Color the water areas around the continents blue.

3. Carefully cut out each continent along the bold lines.

4. Cut out the compass rose. You may color it if you like.

5. On a piece of blue paper 12″ × 18″ arrange the continents to make a map of the world. (HINT: Antarctica goes along the bottom edge.)

6. Paste the continents in place.

7. Paste the compass rose in the lower left-hand corner of your map to show the four compass directions.

Antarctica looks like a strip because the world is round and your map is flat!

Cut out the labels below. Paste them to your world map to name each of the four oceans and seven continents of the world.

NORTH AMERICA	SOUTH AMERICA	ANTARCTICA
AUSTRALIA	AFRICA	EUROPE
ASIA	PACIFIC OCEAN	ATLANTIC OCEAN
INDIAN OCEAN	ARCTIC OCEAN	

Mixed-up Continents

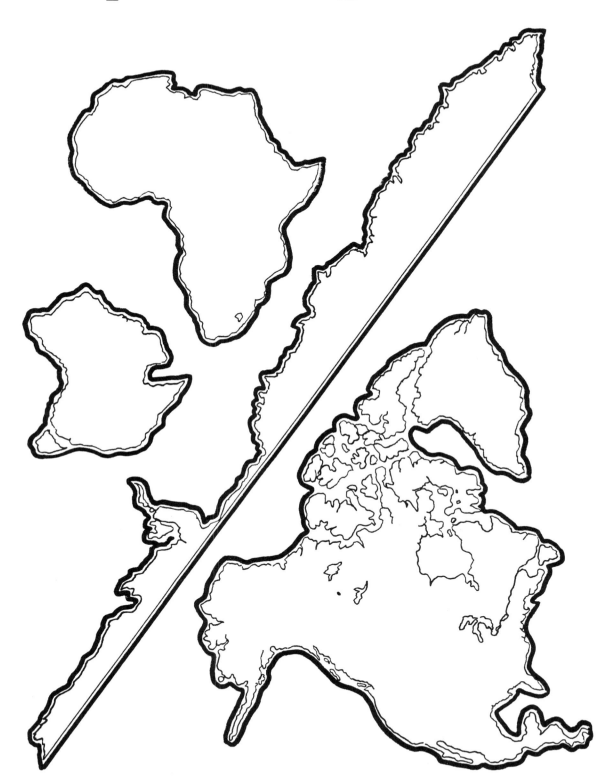

Mixed-up Continents

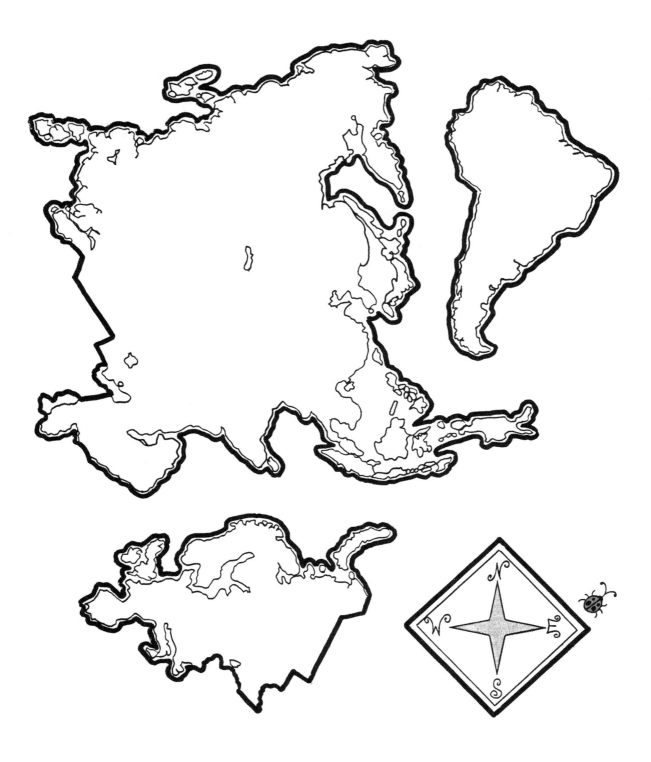

North America Map

1. Label the four edges of your map; NORTH, SOUTH, EAST and WEST.

2. Label the PACIFIC OCEAN, the ATLANTIC OCEAN, the ARCTIC OCEAN, and the GULF OF MEXICO.

3. Color the water on your map blue. (Don't forget about the GREAT LAKES and HUDSON BAY.)

4. Label CANADA and color it green.

5. Label MEXICO and color it brown.

6. Label CENTRAL AMERICA and color it orange.

7. Make a black dot (•) to show where LOS ANGELES, CALIFORNIA, is. Label it.

8. Make a dot for CHICAGO, ILLINOIS, and label it.

9. Mark and label NEW YORK, NEW YORK.

10. Make a red star to show where you live.

11. Color the UNITED STATES yellow. (Remember ALASKA is part of the U.S.)

Fill in the blanks to make a story about where you live.

My name is _____. The country that I live in is

_____. My state is named _____.

_____ is the name of the city nearest my home. Where I live is special

because _____

_____.

Name _____

North America

HAWAII

Criss-cross the Globe

As you read this story, circle the correct word in each numbered box at the bottom of this sheet.

Two kinds of special lines criss-cross the globe. These 1. _____ help to locate places on the globe. The 2. _____ kinds of lines are lines of latitude and lines 3. _____ longitude.

Lines of latitude circle the 4. _____ east and west. They are called parallels of latitude. Parallels of 5. _____ are parallel to the equator. Latitude tells how far a place is north or south of the equator. Latitude 6. _____ measured in degrees. The border between 7. _____ and the western United States is 49° N Latitude. That means it runs along the 49th parallel 8. _____ of the equator.

Lines of longitude are called meridians. Meridians of 9. _____ run between the north and south poles. Meridians of longitude measure east 10. _____ west of the prime meridian. The prime meridian passes through Great Britain. Alaska borders Canada's Yukon Territory along a line 141° W Longitude. That means their border is 141 meridians west of the prime meridian.

© 1989 by The Center for Applied Research in Education, Inc.

What is the Latitude and Longitude of the place where you live?

1.	2.	3.	4.	5.
cross lines globe	two five one	of at from	moon sun globe	globe earth latitude
6.	7.	8.	9.	10.
can weren't is	Brazil Canada Australia	east north west	parallel longitude globes	down and but

Name _____

Latitude Math

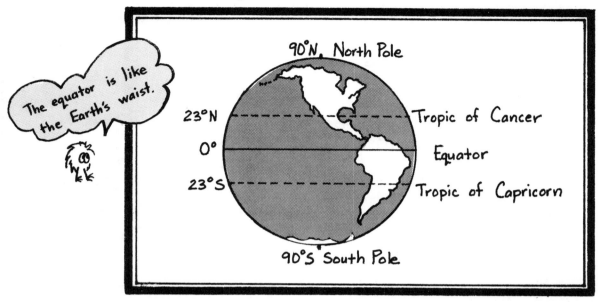

Work Space

1) How many degrees of latitude are between the two tropics?

The Tropic of Cancer is _____ °N.

The Tropic of Capricorn is _____ °S.

The Tropic of Cancer is _____ ° from the Tropic of Capricorn.

2) How many degrees between the North Pole and the Tropic of Capricorn?

3) How many degrees between the Tropic of Cancer and the North Pole?

4) Chicago is about 42°N. How many degrees are between the North Pole and Chicago?

1)

2)

3)

4)

Bonus Box: How many degrees of latitude are between you and the North Pole? (Hint: Use a map to find the latitude of your city.)

Geography—Regions

Look for each of these words in the wordsearch. The words can be found either across or down.

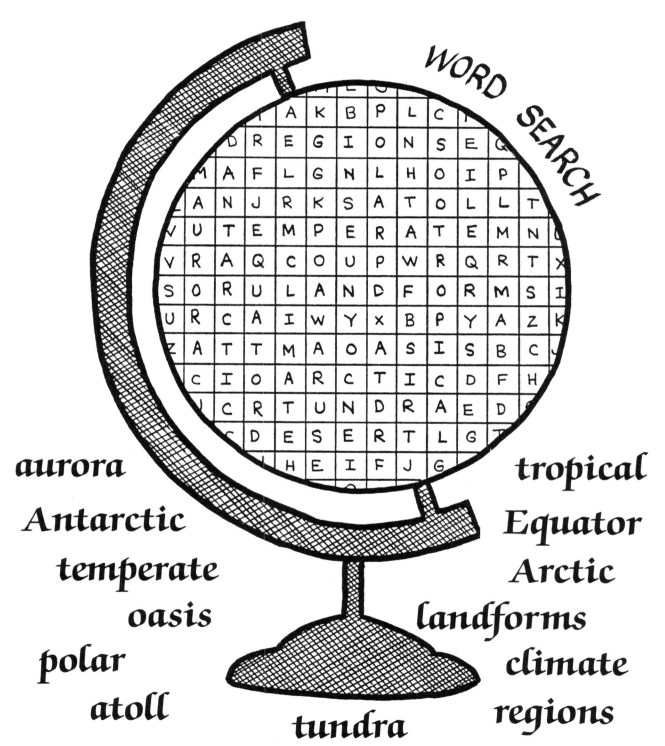

WORD SEARCH

	A	K	B	P	L	C		
D	R	E	G	I	O	N	S	E
A	F	L	G	N	L	H	O	I	P
A	N	J	R	K	S	A	T	O	L	L	T
U	T	E	M	P	E	R	A	T	E	M	N
R	A	Q	C	O	U	P	W	R	Q	R	T
S	O	R	U	L	A	N	D	F	O	R	M	S
R	C	A	I	W	Y	X	B	P	Y	A	Z
A	T	T	M	A	O	A	S	I	S	B	C
C	I	O	A	R	C	T	I	C	D	F	H
C	R	T	U	N	D	R	A	E	D
D	E	S	E	R	T	L	G
H	E	I	F	J	G

aurora

Antarctic

temperate

oasis

polar

atoll

tundra

tropical

Equator

Arctic

landforms

climate

regions

Name _____

WORLD REGIONS CROSSWORD

Grid contains: T E M P E R A T E (with E below)

ACROSS

5. The Tropic of Cancer is located in the northern _____ .

7. The bleak, treeless land in the polar region is called the _____ .

10. The measurement of how hot or cold something is, is its _____ .

12. A ring-shaped coral island is an _____ .

14. A tiny animal whose skeleton forms tropical reefs is _____ .

15. A line of latitude not far from the North Pole is the _____ Circle.

16. An _____ in a desert is where there is water so plants can grow.

17. The type of weather a place usually has is its _____ .

DOWN

1. A region with very little rainfall and few plants is a _____ .

3. _____ tells you how far north or south of the Equator a place is.

4. The directions on a compass are _____ , south, east, and west.

6. The line dividing the northern and southern hemispheres is the _____ .

8. Arctic soil whose lower layers are permanently frozen is _____ .

9. A crack in the earth where hot rock is forced out is a _____ .

11. A product of the Earth that man can use is called a _____ .

13. The _____ of Capricorn is in the southern hemisphere.

Name _____

World Regions

A globe or map of the earth shows us the regions of our world. These regions can be divided into three groups; Polar Regions, Temperate Regions, and Tropical Regions. Each of the earth's regions have many things about them that are alike such as plant and animal life, landforms, and climate. And they also have many differences.

FOLLOW THE DIRECTIONS AND USE THE DRAWING BELOW TO LOCATE THE THREE MAIN REGIONS OF THE WORLD.

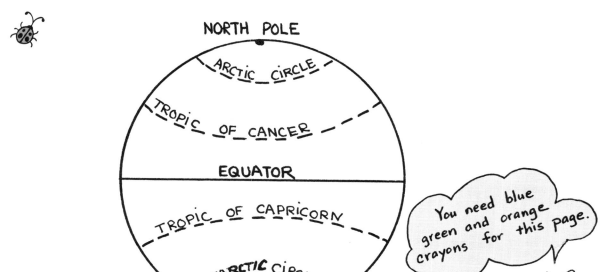

1. Begin by locating the North Pole. From the North Pole to the Arctic Circle is called the North Polar Region. Color the North Polar Region *blue*.

2. Next, locate the South Pole. The area from the South Pole to the Antarctic Circle is called the South Polar Region. Color the South Polar Region *blue*.

3. In the Northern Hemisphere from the Arctic Circle to the Tropic of Cancer is an area we call a Temperate Region. Color this area *green*.

4. In the Southern Hemisphere from the Antarctic Circle to the Tropic of Capricorn is another Temperate Region. Color this area *green*.

5. The middle part of your drawing from the Tropic of Cancer, south past the Equator, to the Tropic of Capricorn makes up the area of the world that we call the Tropical Region. Color this area *orange*.

The colors blue, green, and orange that you have used to color your drawing can help you learn something about the climate and temperatures in each of these regions of the world.

Another way to look at the Polar, Temperate, and Tropical Regions is by looking at the latitude of each region.

FOLLOW THE DIRECTIONS BELOW AND USE THE DRAWING TO LABEL THE LATITUDES OF EACH REGION. WHEN YOU HAVE FINISHED, COLOR THE REGIONS BLUE, GREEN, AND ORANGE.

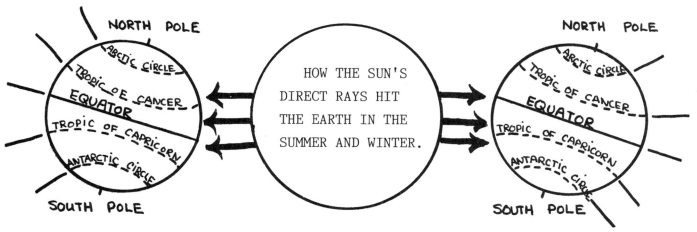

SUMMER IN NORTHERN HEMISPHERE
WINTER IN SOUTHERN HEMISPHERE

WINTER IN NORTHERN HEMISPHERE
SUMMER IN SOUTHERN HEMISPHERE

1. The Equator divides the earth into two equal parts: the Northern and the Southern Hemispheres. The Equator is 0° latitude. Write 0° on the Equator.

2. The Polar Regions are located in areas of high latitude. From the Arctic Circle to the North Pole is the North Polar Region. Write 90°N at the North Pole and 66°N at the Arctic Circle on both drawings.

3. From the Antarctic Circle to the South Pole is the South Polar Region. Write 90°S at the South Pole and 66°S at the Antarctic Circle. High latitude regions like the Polar Region have cold temperatures all year round because they never have the sun's direct rays at any time during the year.

4. The middle latitude areas are the Temperate Regions. There are two Temperate Regions. The North Temperate Region is found from the Tropic of Cancer to the Arctic Circle. Write 23°N on the Tropic of Cancer on both drawings.

5. From the Tropic of Capricorn to the Antarctic Circle is the South Temperate Region. Write 23°S on the Tropic of Capricorn. Middle latitude areas are the Temperate Region. These regions have cold and warm seasons because they get more direct sun rays during some times of the year.

6. Low latitude areas of the earth are the Tropical Region. They begin at the Equator and go North to the Tropic of Cancer and South to the Tropic of Capricorn. Most low latitude places have warm temperatures all year because they get the most direct light from the sun.

Equinox and Solstice

Each year is divided into four season: spring, summer, fall, and winter. The length of the day and the angle at which the sun's rays strike the earth tell us about the seasons in the different regions of the world. As the earth revolves around the sun, it changes its position in relation to the sun. This is why summer is warmer than winter. The seasons in the Northern Hemisphere are just the opposite of those in the Southern Hemisphere.

In the Northern Hemisphere, June 21st is called the *summer solstice*. During this time the sun is the greatest distance away from the Equator. It is the first day of summer. On the summer solstice, all of the region above the Arctic Circle will have 24 hours of sunlight.

December 21st is called the *winter solstice*. Again it is the time when the sun is the greatest distance away from the Equator. It is the first day of winter. On the day of the winter solstice, all of the region above the Arctic Circle will have 24 hours of darkness.

September 22nd is called the *autumn equinox*. March 21st is called the *spring equinox*. On both of these days, the beginning of autumn and the beginning of spring, day and night are equal. They are both 12 hours long.

THINK ABOUT THE SEASONS OF THE YEAR BEING THE OPPOSITE OF EACH OTHER IN THE NORTHERN AND SOUTHERN HEMISPHERES. THEN SEE IF YOU CAN COMPLETE THE CHART BELOW.

NORTHERN HEMISPHERE	*SOUTHERN HEMISPHERE*
Longest day_____	Longest day_____
Shortest day_____	Shortest day_____
Spring begins_____	Spring begins_____
Fall begins_____	Fall begins_____

ON THE NEXT PAGE ARE DRAWINGS OF A TREE FOR EACH OF THE FOUR SEASONS IN THE NORTHERN HEMISPHERE. IF THIS TREE WERE NEAR WHERE YOU LIVE, HOW WOULD IT LOOK DURING EACH OF THE SEASONS? COMPLETE THE DRAWING OF EACH TREE AND USE THE INFORMATION FROM YOUR CHART TO FILL IN THE CORRECT DATES.

Name _____

Seasons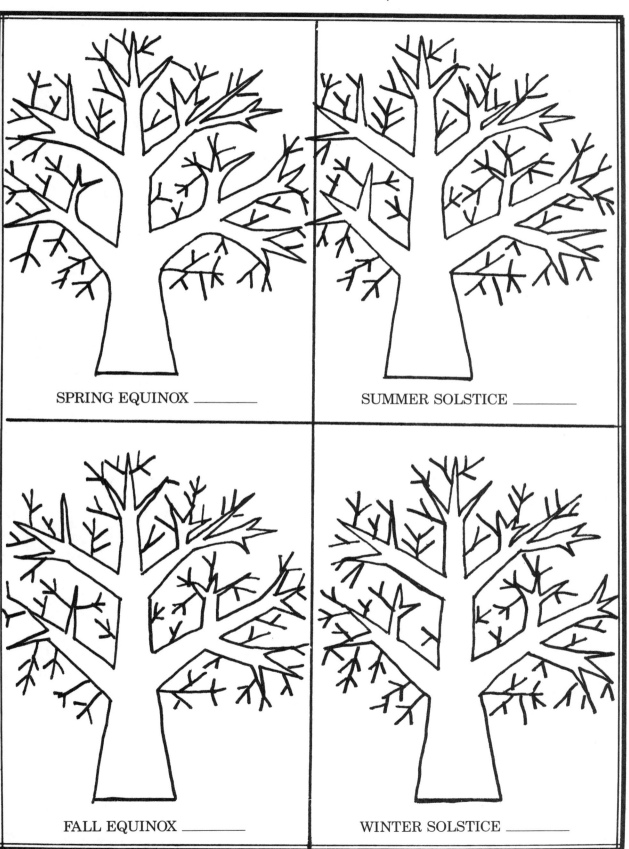

SPRING EQUINOX _____

SUMMER SOLSTICE _____

FALL EQUINOX _____

WINTER SOLSTICE _____

Name _____

All About the Arctic Region

 *Ready:*

masses
tundra
permafrost
active zone
thaws
spongy
lichens
caribou
lemming
voles

1. Small rodents that are members of the rat family are _____ .

2. When something melts after being frozen it _____ .

3. The root or base word for spongy is _____ .

4. A level treeless plain found in the Arctic Region is a _____ .

5. _____ is soil that is permanently frozen.

6. _____ are moss-like plants that grow in the summer on the tundra.

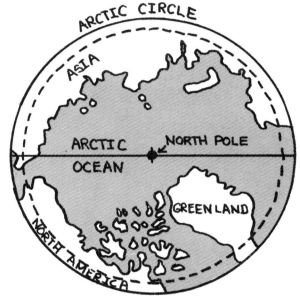

 *Set:*

The North Pole is as far North as you can travel on the earth. The North Pole is not a continent. It is made of large ice masses. The North Pole is surrounded by the Arctic Ocean. The Arctic Ocean is an ice covered ocean with thousands of islands. The northern edges of Europe, Asia, and North America touch the Arctic Ocean and are part of the Arctic Polar Region.

The land around the Arctic Ocean is very different from the land where you live. Much of the land is tundra. Tundra is land on soil where it is too cold for trees to grow. The ground is frozen almost all year long. This soil is called permafrost because it is permanently frozen. The greatest recorded depth of permafrost was reported in Russia at 4,920 feet.

The upper layer of permafrost is called the active zone. The active zone thaws only in the summer. In some parts of the Arctic Region the layer of permafrost is thin. Here, in the spring time, the warm sun thaws the soil near the earth's surface. The soil below the surface stays frozen so that water cannot be soaked up. This makes the ground feel wet and spongy. Insects like flies, mosquitoes, bees, and butterflies appear during the summer months. The thawing allows small plants such as moss and lichens to grow. These plants grow close to the ground and have short roots. Over 1,700 kinds of plants including 900 kinds of flowers grow in the Arctic Region.

The most common animals in the Arctic Region are the reindeer and the caribou. Large herds of these animals roam the pastures feeding on the Arctic grasses of the tundra. Bears, foxes, rabbits, and squirrels are found in the Arctic Region. Small mouse-like creatures such as lemmings and voles also provide food for the larger animals. Almost all of these animals live and feed near the water's edge along the shores of the Arctic Ocean.

Many kinds of water mammals and fish are found in the Arctic Ocean. Seals, whales, porpoises, dolphins, and walruses live here. Eskimo hunters and fishermen have made their homes in the Arctic Region for over 10,000 years.

 Go:

1. What is the northernmost place on earth?_____

2. How many continents touch the Arctic Ocean? Circle one number. 3 5 7

3. Land on soil where it is too cold for trees to grow is called _____ .

4. Name two mouse-like creatures that provide food for other larger animals that live

   in the Arctic Region are _____ and _____ .

5. Land that is always frozen is called permafrost. Yes _____ or No _____ .

6. In the last paragraph, what group of people have hunted and fished in the Arctic

   Region for thousands of years? _____.

How Cold Is It?

The numbers on this chart show the temperatures in the Arctic and the Antarctic Regions for one year. Water freezes at 32 degrees above 0. The temperatures above 0 degrees have no minus (−) sign. Temperatures below 0 degrees on the chart are shown by a minus (−) sign placed before the number. Use this chart to answer the questions below.

TEMPERATURES IN THE POLAR REGIONS

ARCTIC REGION–NORTH POLE

Jan.	Feb.	Mar.	Apr.	May	June	July	Aug.	Sept.	Oct.	Nov.	Dec.
−14	−12	−19	−7	15	30	35	34	29	14	−2	−12

ANTARCTIC REGION–SOUTH POLE

Jan.	Feb.	Mar.	Apr.	May	June	July	Aug.	Sept.	Oct.	Nov.	Dec.
−24	−48	−69	−83	−81	−90	−86	−97	−87	−74	−46	−28

1. What is the coldest temperature in the Arctic Region? The coldest temperature was

   _____ degrees in the month of _____ .

2. What was the coldest temperature in the Antarctic Region? The coldest tempera-

   ture was _____ degrees in the month of _____ .

3. What are the three (3) *coldest* months in the Arctic Region? The three coldest

   months are _____ , _____ , and _____ .

4. What are the three (3) *warmest* months in the Antarctic Region? The three

   warmest months are _____ , _____ , and _____ .

5. Why are the three coldest months in the Arctic Region about the same as the three

   warmest months in the Anarctic Region?_____

   _____

6. Which region is warmer all year?_____

7. Which region is colder all year?_____

★ BONUS: What are the yearly average temperatures for each region? Ask your teacher to show you how to solve this problem.

Name _____

Eskimos

As you read this story, circle the correct word in each numbered box at the bottom of this sheet.

The Eskimos live in the cold, treeless Arctic Regions. Their homes are found in Asia, North America, and Greenland. The

1. _____ Eskimo means "eaters of raw meat." Northern Eskimos call themselves "Innuit' which means "men" in the Eskimo language.

The Eskimo way of life is a mixture of 2. _____ ways and new ways. Today many live in communities, work at jobs, and go to school just like 3. _____ . In the past their lives were much different.

The ancestors of the Eskimos probably came from Asia 4. _____ thousand years ago. They did not live in tribes like the North American Indians. They 5. _____ in family settlements and traveled across the Arctic Region in 6. _____ of food. They often had two homes—one temporary one for summer and one permanent one for winter. We usually think that Eskimos lived only in 7. _____ . But this is not true. Most often their homes were made out of whatever 8. _____ were available. Some were wooden, but many were made from sod.

The Eskimos got most of their food from the sea. They ate seals, fish, walruses, whales, 9. _____ sea birds. They hunted caribou on the land. The Eskimos often ate their food raw because they did not have fuel needed for cooking. Their food was always

10. _____ by everyone in their family settlement. All parts of the creatures they fished and hunted for were used for food, clothing, and tools.

1.	2.	3.	4.	5.
word	new	me	several	worked
called	strange	I	hundreds	lived
game	old	you	tens	plan
6.	**7.**	**8.**	**9.**	**10.**
hunting	igloos	building	and	ate
search	tents	ice	near	shared
catching	apartments	materials	hunted	worn

Name _____

 *Ready:*

snowhouse
shelter
extreme
temporary
sod
chink
igloo
blubber
semisubterranean
material

1. The word that has the same "oo" sound as "hoot" is _____ .

2. Earth with grass growing in it is called _____ .

3. _____ means to fill in cracks.

4. _____ is a compound word.

5. Permanent means the opposite of _____ .

6. The word that has seven syllables is _____ .

7. The thick fat from a whale is called _____ .

 *Set:*

ARCTIC HOMES

In the arctic regions, the temperature sometimes gets as low as 60° below 0. The Eskimos build comfortable houses to keep them warm and dry. Since there are no trees, the Eskimos must use whatever material they can find. They build their houses out of stones, earth or even snow!

"Igloo" is the Eskimo word for house. Igloos made of sod or stones are called "innies." The Eskimos also build homes that are partly underground. They use driftwood, stones and earth to build these semisubterranean houses. Moss is used to chink, or fill, the cracks to keep out the wind and cold. The roof is covered with earth to keep the house warm. Inside, a platform covered with fur hides or grass is used for sitting and sleeping. Whale blubber lamps supply light and heat.

If the Eskimos need temporary shelter from extreme cold, they may build a snowhouse. These igloos are made of blocks cut from frozen snow with a knife made of steel or whale-bone. Smaller blocks of snow are stacked on top of larger ones and the cracks between are packed with snow. A hole is left in the top of the igloo to let in fresh air. Instead of a door, the snowhouse has a long, low tunnel. This low entrance helps keep out the cold. The opening is covered with an animal skin.

We can see from their homes, that the Eskimos have adapted well to a harsh land. They have learned to use the scarce natural resources of their environment. These skills help the Eskimos to live comfortably in the frozen arctic regions.

Go:

1. _____ is the Eskimo word for "house."

2. Instead of a door, a snowhouse has a long, low (roof, window, tunnel)

3. The temperature in the arctic regions is sometimes 60° below 0. (Yes, No)

4. Steel or _____ knives are used to cut frozen snow into blocks.

5. A house that is built partly underground of driftwood, earth and stone is a _____ house.

6. Eskimos use little wood in their houses because there are no _____ in the arctic.

All About the Antarctic Region

 *Ready:*

continents
surround
constantly
average
icecap
resources
interior
lifeless
permanent
research

1. A compound word that means a mass of ice usually over a large area is an _____ .

2. The opposite of temporary is _____ .

3. _____ are large land masses in the globe.

4. Temperature that is typical or normal is _____ .

5. The _____ or inland area of Antarctica is lifeless.

6. _____ means to study or investigate facts to gain information.

 *Set:*

The South Pole is as far South as you can travel on earth. The South Pole is located on the continent of Antarctica. Antarctica is shaped like a big cookie. It is about twice as big as the continent of Australia. Three oceans, the Atlantic, the Pacific, and the Indian Ocean, surround the continent of Antarctica.

Antarctica is the coldest land on earth. Two-hundred-mile-an-hour winds with dry, cold air blow constantly. Although the air is dry and cold, there is little snow. The South Pole only gets about four to six inches of new snow each

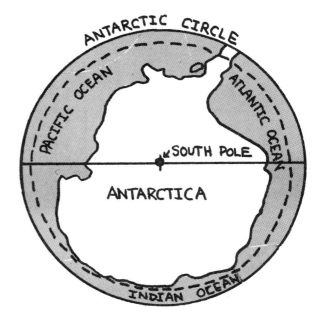

year. The average temperature in Antarctica is below 0°F all year. In the summer the temperature might reach 32°F. The lowest temperature ever recorded on earth was in Vostok, Antarctica. It was −126.9°F!

Most of the land of Antarctica is buried under a mile-thick icecap. Mountain peaks stick up out of the ice and snow. Huge glaciers move from mountain valleys to the oceans.

In fact, if this giant icecap ever melted, Antarctica would be a continent of mountain islands.

Antarctica has few natural resources. But, the seacoast has many kinds of animal life. Millions of seals, thousands of whales, fish, penguins, and other birds depend on the sea for food and shelter. Only a few kinds of plants and insects live on the rocky hillsides along the ocean shores. The interior region of Antarctica is lifeless.

Until recent times, no people have ever lived permanently on the continent of Antarctica. Whale and seal hunters began hunting in Antarctica in the early 1800s. Elephant seals weighing over four tons and Blue Whales weighing over 150 tons were killed. Today there are laws that limit the number of seals and whales that can be killed each year.

Scientists now go to Antarctica to do research and explore the region around the South Pole. One of the interesting things these scientists have found are fossils of plants and petrified wood. This leads them to believe that millions of years ago Antarctica was a warmer land covered with trees and plants.

Go:

1. The South Pole is located on the continent of _____ .

2. Named the three oceans that surround Antarctica. _____ , _____ , and _____ .

3. How much snow does the South Pole get during an average year? Circle one.

   4 to 6 feet   4 to 6 inches   4 to 6 meters

4. The largest creature to have ever lived on earth is the _____ .

   Choose one.   elephant seal   dinosaur   blue whale

5. There are no plants or animals living in the interior of Antarctica.

   Yes _____ or No _____

6. What two kinds of evidence have scientists found that lead them to believe

   Antarctica was once a warmer land? _____ and _____ .

The blue whale is the largest animal that ever lived.

Name _____

What is an Aurora?

As you read this story, circle the correct word in each numbered box at the bottom of this sheet.

The Earth is like a giant magnet. On Earth the energy is strongest at the poles. The Earth's magnetic 1. _____ are not exactly at the North Pole or the South Pole. They are about 1,200 miles away.

Each year 2. _____ the spring and fall glowing sheets of bright colored lights appear in the 3. _____ sky. Sometimes they look like long streamers of light. At other times they look like huge colored waterfalls or curtains of light 4. _____ from outer space. These natural light shows of color 5. _____ called auroras.

Auroras begin with the sun. In the spring and fall the sun shoots 6. _____ atomic particles that travel rapidly through 7. _____ . When these particles near the Earth, they move toward the magnetic poles. As they enter the Earth's 8. _____ , they collide with the atoms of air. These collisions create the energy that makes the sky glow.

In the northern Arctic Region these beautiful displays of 9. _____ are called the Aurora Borealis or the Northern Lights. The black night sky shines with green, yellow, pink, and purple light. In the 10. _____ Antarctic Region these "fireworks" in they sky are called the Aurora Australis and they usually glow a pale green color.

© 1989 by The Center for Applied Research in Education, Inc.

1.	2.	3.	4.	5.
places	during	daytime	near	are
poles	while	night	crash	aren't
kinds	over	sunny	falling	is
6.	7.	8.	9.	10.
off	Earth	night	darkness	southern
on	solar	atmosphere	storms	western
fly	space	day	light	northern

Name _____

Handwriting—The Tropics

The tropics cover the area within about 1600 miles of the equator.

hemisphere

islands

coral

atoll

Oceania

deserts

volcanoes

temperature

degrees

rainfall

Name _____

All About the Tropical Region

 *Ready:*

| driest |
| coral |
| atoll |
| sunken |
| evergreen |
| volcanoes |
| desert |
| temperature |
| degree |
| unusual |

1. An _____ is a ring-shaped coral island.

2. A compound word that means always green is _____ .

3. A _____ is a unit of measurement used for things like latitude, longitude, and temperature.

4. A tiny little animal that lives in warm ocean waters and whose skeleton forms reefs and islands is _____.

5. The measurement of how hot or cold something is is its _____ .

6. The word formed from the root or base word <u>dry</u> would be _____ .

Set:

The Tropical Region of the World is located on both sides of the Equator from the Tropic of Cancer to the Tropic of Capricorn. Within the Tropical Region are thousands of islands, rain forests, and deserts. Here you will find some of the hottest, wettest, and driest places on earth.

Oceania or the "water hemisphere" is the name given to the thousands of islands scattered across the Pacific Ocean. Many of these islands are coral atolls. They are formed around the rims of sunken volcanoes. The Oceania area gets large amounts of rainfall and it is almost always warm.

The "rain forest" is the name given to another part of the Tropical Region. The "rain forests" are located close to the Equator in South America, Africa, and Southeast Asia. These areas often get between 100 and 150 inches of rain each year. With these large amounts of rain and the warm temperatures, plants and trees grow closely together. Over 3,000 different kinds of evergreen plants and trees cover the land of the "rain forests."

Not all parts of the Tropical Region are warm and wet. Part of the Tropical Region is desert. The deserts of South America, Africa, Southeast Asia, and Australia have no more than five to ten inches of rain each year. The daily temperatures are often above 100° degrees.

In many parts of the Tropical Region, the temperatures stay about the same twelve months of the year. Along the Equator the temperatures at night may only be ten to fifteen degrees cooler than in the daytime. But, it is not unusual in the winter months for temperatures in the desert areas to be above 90° degrees in the daytime and drop to 35° to 40° degrees at night. That is cold enough for frost to form at night!

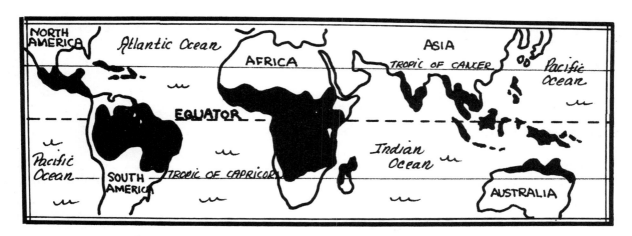

 Go:

1. The Tropical Region is located on both sides of the _____ .

2. What is the name given to the thousands of islands in the Pacific Ocean? Two

   possible answers. _____ or _____ _____ .

3. Coral skeletons for reefs and islands. Coral is a volcano, plant, or an animal. Circle the correct answer.

4. How much rain might fall each year in the "rain forest" areas of the Tropical Region? Circle one. 10 to 20 inches   100 to 150 inches   5 to 10 inches

5. Desert areas of the Tropical Region may get only five to ten inches of rain each year.

   Yes _____ or No_____

6. In which part of the Tropical Region would you find the most plants and trees?

   _____

Name _____

What is an Atoll?

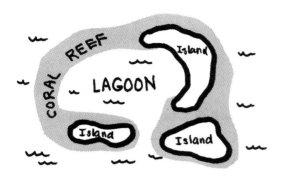

As you read this story, circle the correct word in each numbered box at the bottom of the sheet.

In the warm waters near the Equator, there live millions of tiny animals called coral polyps. Coral polyps are only about a fraction of an 1. _____ long. They have cylinder-shaped bodies. At the top of the body is the mouth with tiny tentacles for catching 2. _____ . The bottom part of the coral polyp attaches itself to hard underwater surfaces like the rims of sunken volcanoes on the sea bottom. If the 3. _____ is shallow, the coral polyps attach themselves to each other and live in 4. _____ colonies.

The coral polyp feeds and builds up its limestone skeleton by taking calcium from the sea water. It deposits limestone around the lower half of its body. When the coral polyps die, the limestone "skeletons" are 5. _____ and new polyps attach themselves. Over millions of 6. _____ of time limestone formations build up coral reefs and islands 7. _____ sea level.

An atoll is a small coral island. It is built up on a 8. _____ volcano. Atolls are usually formed in the shape of a ring. In the center of the 9. _____ is a lagoon. Channels connect the lagoon to the sea on the windward side of the island. Thin layers of soil lodge on the coral island and tropical plant life begins to grow. Breadfruit, taro, and coconut grow. These foods, along with fish from the sea provide food for the small groups of people who live on 10. _____ islands.

1.	2.	3.	4.	5.
foot	nets	coral	coral	went
yard	food	animals	shell	gone
inch	cold	water	animal	left
6.	7.	8.	9.	10.
days	up	sunken	shaped	each
years	above	erupting	near	atoll
weeks	high	active	ring	huge

Name _____

Coconuts

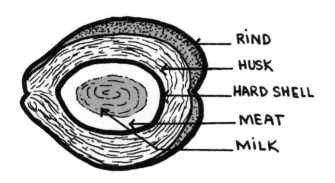

RIND
HUSK
HARD SHELL
MEAT
MILK

As you read this story, circle the correct word in each numbered box at the bottom of the sheet.

Coconuts come from the coconut palm tree. Coconut palm trees grow to be 40 to 100 feet high. They need year round warm temperatures, plenty of moisture, and lots of sunshine to grow. Coconut palms have no branches. Their large leaves grow out from the top of the 1. _____ . The 2. _____ is the fruit of the coconut palm tree. A healthy tree produces about 100 coconuts each year.

The outside of the coconut has a smooth light-colored rind. Under the rind is a thick layer of brownish-red fiber 3. _____ the husk. The rind and the husk cover a hard brown shell. Inside the 4. _____ is the seed. The seed has a hollow in the center and is filled with a sweet liquid called the milk.

The oily 5. _____ coconut meat of the seed and the milk are staple foods of many tropical people. Coconut meat can be eaten raw or dried. Oil is squeezed from the 6. _____ and used for cooking. Oil is also traded and used for making margarine, salad oils, soap, and even lipstick. The milk makes a delicious 7. _____ . Children like to eat the sweet coconut shoots much like you might eat a candy 8. _____ .

The coconut palm tree does more than just provide food. Cleaned out shells become cups and spoons. Fibers from the 9. _____ are twisted to make rope and twine. The flat feather-like leaves are used to thatch roofs of houses. Twine and leaves are 10. _____ into mats and baskets. Even the trunks of trees are used as wood for building bridges, homes, and furniture.

1.	2.	3.	4.	5.
tree	leaf	over	husk	brown
stems	palm	called	shell	pink
leaves	coconut	near	rind	white
6.	7.	8.	9.	10.
meat	dinner	juice	husk	pounded
shell	fruit	bar	rind	stretched
food	drink	bread	shell	woven

Hawaii and Puerto Rico

Hawaii is called the "island state." It is one of the 50 United States. It is the only state that is not on the mainland of North America. Hawaii is made up of hundred of islands that cover 6,424 square miles in the Pacific Ocean.

The Hawaiian Islands were formed millions of years ago by volcanoes under the ocean. Two of these volcanoes are still active today. Hawaii has dry desert like areas and wet tropical rain forests. The climate is warm with lots of sunshine and lots of rain. The daily temperatures in Hawaii are almost the same in summer and winter. The weather changes in Hawaii are caused by winds that blow from the Pacific Ocean toward the Equator. They are called "Trade Winds." Northeast winds pick up moisture from the ocean. As the winds near the mountains, they lose their moisture in the form of rain.

Tourism is the biggest industry in Hawaii today. There are also many large sugarcane and pineapple plantations in Hawaii. If you look at the labels from sugar and pineapple containers, you will probably see that they come from Hawaii.

Puerto Rico and Hawaii are alike in many ways. The name Puerto Rico means "rich port" in Spanish. Puerto Rico is not a state, but its people are United States citizens. They follow the same laws that we do. Someday they may choose to become the 51st state in the United States.

Puerto Rico is an island in the Atlantic Ocean about 1,000 miles from Florida. It covers 3,435 square miles. Like Hawaii, it is near the Equator. This island was not formed by volcanoes. It is the peak of a huge mountain range that rises from beneath the sea.

The climate in Puerto Rico is mild and the daily weather is very much like that of Hawaii. The Trade Winds blow from the Atlantic Ocean across Puerto Rico. In the rainforest areas they may have 180 inches of rain each year.

Sugarcane is the most important crop in Puerto Rico. Coffee is the second most important crop. Tourism is a big business. There are also many factories that manufacture clothing, machinery, chemicals, and medicines.

Name _____

Compare the Facts

Time to compare the facts about Hawaii and Puerto Rico. Read the list of facts in the box below. Write the letter for each fact in the correct place on the chart at the bottom of the page. Two facts belong on both Hawaii and Puerto Rico.

Sugar Cane

A. The "island state"

B. 1,000 miles from Florida

C. means "rich port" in Spanish

D. not a state, but people are U.S. citizens

E. 50th state in the U.S.

F. has two active volcanoes

G. formed by undersea mountain peaks

H. has sugarcane plantations

I. has pineapple plantations

J. tourism is an important industry

K. coffee is the second most important crop

L. located in the Pacific Ocean

M. located in the Atlantic Ocean

N. gets heavy rain from the Trade Winds

O. has the largest number of square miles

Hawaii

1. _____
2. _____
3. _____
4. _____
5. _____
6. _____
7. _____
8. _____
9. _____
10. _____
_____

Puerto Rico

1. _____
2. _____
3. _____
4. _____
5. _____
6. _____
7. _____
8. _____
9. _____
10. _____
_____

YOU SHOULD HAVE 9 FACTS FOR HAWAII AND 9 FACTS FOR PUERTO RICO. SEE IF YOU CAN THINK OF ONE MORE FACT FOR EACH ISLAND AND WRITE THEM ON THE LINES.

Name ——————————

You're A Winner!

WESTERN UNION

CONGRATULATIONS!!!!!!!!!!! PACK YOUR BAGS FOR A TRIP TO THE TROPICS .... YOU HAVE JUST WON AN ALL-EXPENSE PAID TRIP TO THE BEAUTIFUL ISLAND OF HAWAII. A CHAUFFEUR DRIVEN LIMOUSINE WILL PICK YOU UP IN EXACTLY ONE HOUR TO TAKE YOU TO THE AIRPORT. YOU MUST QUICKLY MAKE A LIST OF THINGS TO TAKE WITH YOU IN YOUR SUITCASE. LIST AS MANY THINGS AS YOU CAN THAT YOU WANT TO HAVE WITH YOU ON YOUR TROPICAL VACATION. YOU HAVE FIVE MINUTES TO MAKE YOUR LIST. READY? SET? GO! .... STOP AFTER FIVE MINUTES AND COMPARE YOUR LIST WITH YOUR CLASSMATES'.

TELEGRAM

© 1989 by The Center for Applied Research in Education, Inc.

How many things did you pack? ————— Name one important thing that you forgot to put in your suitcase. ————— If your trip has all the expenses paid for you, would you need to bring along any money? ————— Why? ———————————————————————

Name _____

All About the Sahara Desert

 *Ready:*

deserts yearly recorded edges oasis underground nomad sources adapted channel

1. A _____ is a body of water that brings water to dry desert lands.

2. The plural form of this word is oases. What is the singular word form of oases? _____

3. The compound word that means below the ground is _____ .

4. Something that happens annually happens _____ .

5. A _____ is a person who moves from place to place in search of food and water.

6. Animals that have found ways of surviving on the hot deserts have _____ .

3,250,000 SQUARE MILES!

 *Set:*

Most of the world's deserts are found in the Tropical Region. These deserts lie near the Tropic of Cancer in the north and the Tropic of Capricorn in the south.

The Sahara Desert in Africa is the largest desert in the world. It is almost as large as all of the United States. It is one of the driest places on earth. The average yearly rainfall of the Sahara Desert is about two inches. The highest temperature ever recorded in the world was 136° in the Sahara Desert! Temperatures are not always the same night and day in the desert. The greatest temperature drop ever recorded in a single day also happened in the Sahara Desert. The temperature dropped from 126° to 26°!

Most of the people live along the edges of the Sahara Desert. Here, the winds from the Atlantic Ocean, Mediterranean Sea, and Red Sea provide water in the form of rain. Other people live along the Nile River or near oases. An oasis is a place in the desert where water is collected from underground springs beneath the desert sands. Groups of people called nomads move from one oasis to another across the Sahara Desert in search of food and water.

Along the edges of the Sahara, near the Nile River, and the oases, many kinds of plants and animals are found. But, away from these areas, there are few plants and animals. Water and food sources are scarce. Dust and swirling sand blown by the winds create hundreds of miles of sand dunes. The few plants and animals that live in the desert have adapted so that they need less water to survive. Desert plants store water in their leaves and stems. Camels do not sweat as much as other animals and store water in their bodies.

In the past, people thought that the desert areas were useless. But this is not true. Water channeled by irrigation streams has been brought to the dry land. Plants and animals live there now. More important, the people of the Sahara have found oil beneath the desert sands. Oil drilling rigs pump oil from the ground. Pipelines carry the oil to shipping ports and it is sold all over the world.

A camel can drink 30 gallons of water in 10 min.

 Go:

1. In what region of the world are most of the deserts found? _____ .

2. The Sahara Desert, the largest desert in the world, is located on the continent of

    _____.

    Choose one. South America   Africa   Asia

3. What do we call a place where water is collected from underground springs? This

    place is called an _____ .

4. Are there many food and water sources for man, plants, and animals on the Sahara

    Desert? _____ Yes _____ No

5. What desert plant can you think of that stores food and water in its stems and

    leaves? _____

6. Name the important natural resource that is shipped all over the world that is

    found beneath the desert sands. _____

7. The greatest temperature drop in a single day was recorded on the Sahara Desert.

    How many degrees did it drop on that day? _____

Name _____

All About the Temperate Region

 *Ready:*

climate
latitude
determined
hemisphere
season
opposite
population
located
temperate
direct

1. Something that has been decided has been _____ .

2. Sun rays that point straight down toward the earth are _____ rays.

3. A word that means the number of people who live in an area is _____ .

4. A quarter of a year such as spring, summer, fall, or winter determined by the weather is a _____ .

5. A half of a sphere is called a _____ .

6. The kind of weather that an area has over a long period of time is its _____ .

 *Set:*

Climate is the kind of weather an area has over a long period of time. The climate of a region is determined by its latitude. Low latitude areas get direct rays from the sun near the Equator. The climate is warm. Low latitude areas are the Tropical Region. High latitude areas never get direct rays from the sun. The climate is cold. High latitude areas are the Polar Regions.

In between the Tropical Region and the Polar Regions are the middle latitude areas. The middle latitude areas are called the Temperate Regions of the world. Temperate Regions are found on both sides of the Equator. In the Northern Hemisphere the Temperate Region begins at the Tropic of Cancer and goes to the Arctic Circle. In the Southern Hemisphere the Temperate Region goes from the Tropic of Capricorn to the Antarctic Circle.

Temperate Regions of the world have both warm and cold climates. Temperate Regions have changing seasons—summer, fall, winter, and spring. The seasons in the Temperate Region in the Northern Hemisphere are always the opposite of the seasons of the Temperate Region in the Southern Hemisphere. In the Northern Hemisphere summer comes in June. In the Southern Hemisphere summer comes in January.

If you look at a world map or globe, you will see that most of the land masses of the Temperate Region are located in the Northern Hemisphere. North America, northern Africa, Europe, and Asia are in this Temperate Region. Most of the world's population lives in the Northern Temperate Region. The Temperate Region of the Southern Hemisphere is mostly water—the Pacific Ocean, Atlantic Ocean, and Indian Ocean. Only parts of South America, Africa, and Australia are located in the Southern Temperate Region. There is also much less population in the Southern Temperate Region.

 Go:

1. What determines the climate of a region? Choose one.

        longitude   latitude   hemisphere

2. Which region gets direct rays from the sun?_____

3. Are high latitude areas Polar Regions? Circle one.　Yes　No

4. What are the middle latitude regions called? Choose one.

        Polar Regions   Tropical Regions   Temperate Regions

5. Temperate Regions have changing seasons.　True　False

6. Which region has most of the land masses and population of the world?

   Choose one.   North Temperate Region   South Temperate Region

7. When does summer come in the Southern Hemisphere?_____

   Is this the opposite of where you live?　Yes　No

Name _____

Animals of the Temperate Regions

Hundreds of different kinds of animals make their homes in the Temperate Regions of the world. Some animals are found only in the Northern Temperate Regions. Some are found only in the Southern Temperate Regions. Others might be found in both regions. Look at the silhouette pictures of the animals below. Write the name of each animal below the picture.

1. _____   2. _____   3. _____

4. _____   5. _____   6. _____

Three of the animals above are common in the North Temperate Region. Three of the animals are common in the South Temperate Region. List the animals on the chart below under their correct region. Then, look up ANIMALS in the encyclopedia and see if you can name other animals that are found in each region.

NORTH TEMPERATE REGION	SOUTH TEMPERATE REGION
_____	_____
_____	_____
_____	_____
_____	_____

Name _____

40° Latitude Across the U.S.A.

Different regions of the United States have different climates. The climate of a region is determined by how close a place is to a body of water and by the altitude of the land surface. Altitude means the height of the land above sea level. The higher the altitude of a place, the cooler the temperature.

The United States has many kinds of land surfaces. If you were to take a trip across the land surface at 40° north latitude, the land surface would look like the drawing at the bottom of this page.

Beginning along the west coast near the Pacific Ocean there are high mountain ranges separated by deep valleys. Notice Death Valley on the drawing. Death Valley is the lowest, driest, and hottest place in the United States. Beyond the high mountain ranges are high, almost level, wide plateaus.

Further toward the east are the high rugged peaks of the Rocky Mountains. Denver, Colorado, is located at the base of the Rocky Mountains. It has an elevation of 5,280 feet. East of the Rocky Mountains is a great plain region. Kansas City, Kansas, and Kansas City, Missouri, are located at about 40° latitude as you continue the journey across the United States. Both of these cities are located along the Missouri River.

In the eastern part of the United States is the low mountain region. This region is called the Appalachian Highland. The Appalachian Mountains are lower and not as steep as the mountains in the west. Along the Atlantic Coast is a low coastal plain that extends to the Atlantic Ocean. The capitol of the United States, Washington D.C., is located on the low coastal plain along the Potomac River.

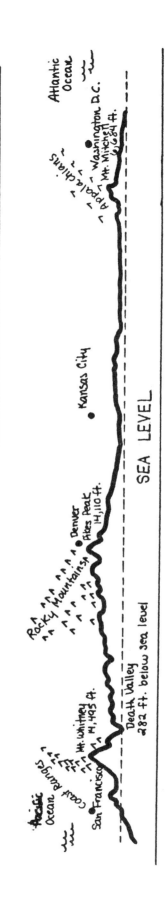

Name _____

40° Latitude Chart

You have completed your trip across the United States at 40° latitude. If you look at a large United States map in your classroom, you will see that colors are used on a map to show elevation. Green is usually used to show a low plains region, yellow represents flat plateau regions, gold or tan represents hills or low mountain regions, and brown is used to represent higher mountain regions. Think about the water and land surfaces you read about. Then see if you can complete the chart below.

City	Color	Land Surfaces	Weather Conditions	Today's Temperature
San Francisco, California				
Death Valley, California				
Denver, Colorado				
Kansas City, Kansas or Missouri				
Washington, D.C.				

To answer the question about today's weather, use the weather report from your local newspaper and record the temperatures for each city.

Regions' Story Problems

1. Six thirsty camels came to an oasis in the Sahara Desert. Each camel drank 30 gallons of water in 10 minutes. How many gallons of water did the six thirsty camels drink all together?

2. Polar explorers made two trips to Antarctica. On their first trip in January the temperature was −24°. On their second trip in August the temperature was −97°. How much colder was it in August than in January?

3. The hundreds of islands that make up Hawaii cover 6,424 square miles. Puerto Rico covers 3,435 square miles. How much larger is Hawaii than Puerto Rico?

4. Death Valley is 282 feet below sea level. Mt. Whitney is 14,495 feet above sea level. What is the total difference in altitude between these two places .... Hint: You have to add. Do you know why?

Name _____

All About Population

 *Ready:*

population
billion
density
evenly
permanent
climate
temperate
business
cluster
transportation

1. One thousand millions makes one _____ .

2. Something that stays all the time is _____ .

3. The _____ regions are between the arctic and tropical regions.

4. Population _____ tells how many people live in how much space.

5. _____ moves people and products from one place to another.

6. The average weather a place has over a long period of time is its _____ .

 *Set:*

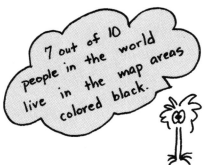

7 out of 10 people in the world live in the map areas colored black.

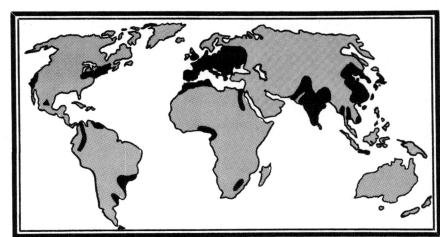

Population means a number of people. It might mean the number of people in a city or country. Population could even mean how many people are in your school or classroom.

The population of the world is more than FIVE BILLION PEOPLE! China has the most people. Its population is more than one billion. The United States has about one quarter as many people as China.

Population density tells how many people share how much space. If people covered the world evenly, 87 people would share each square mile. People do not cover the world evenly.

Some places have many people living closely together. New York City has a high population density. Alaska has a low population density, because few people live in a very large area. Antarctica has no permanent population at all!

One reason people chose to live where they do is climate. First people wanted to live where they could grow food. They settled where the climate was neither too cold nor too hot. Most people live in the temperate regions of the world. Many crops grow well in the temperate regions.

Business is another reason for population to grow. Businesses need many workers. Population clusters around business centers. Business centers often grow near good transportation. Water was the best early transportation. Look at a world population map. Notice how many centers of population are near water routes.

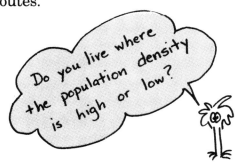

Do you live where the population density is high or low?

 *Go:*

1. _____ means the number of people living in a place.

2. The world population is over (5, 8, 11) billion.

3. People cover the world land surfaces evenly. (YES, NO)

4. Most people live in the _____ regions of the world.

5. Climate is one _____ people choose to live in a place.

6. _____ has no permanent population.

7. New York City has a (high, low) population density.

Name _____

Comparing Regions

Fill in the grid below with facts about the three major world regions.

	TROPICAL REGION	TEMPERATE REGION	ARCTIC REGION
climate			
clothing			
homes			
food			
animals			
plants			

In which region do you live?

Name _____

Geography Quick Check

Use the word box to help you complete the sentences.

seven	longitude	Equator	hemispheres	continents
regions	Temperate	Tropical	four	longitude

1. There are _____ continents on the earth.

2. The Equator divides the earth into northern and southern _____ .

3. Lines of _____ circle the globe east and west.

4. Lines of _____ run from the North Pole to the South Pole.

5. Polar, Temperate, and Tropical are names of _____ of the world.

6. The region located on both sides of the Equator is the _____ region.

7. Middle latitude areas are called the _____ region.

 Write "Yes" for true, and write "No" for not true.

8. ____ Equinoxes and solstices divide the year into seasons.

9. ____ The region closest to the North Pole is the Antarctic Region.

10. ____ The Arctic Region is the coldest land on earth.

11. ____ Hawaii and Puerto Rico are located in the Tropical Region.

12. ____ Most of the world's largest deserts are found in the Temperate Region.

13. ____ An atoll island is formed by tiny animals called coral polyps.

14. ____ The Antarctic Region near the South Pole gets colder than the Arctic Region near the North Pole.

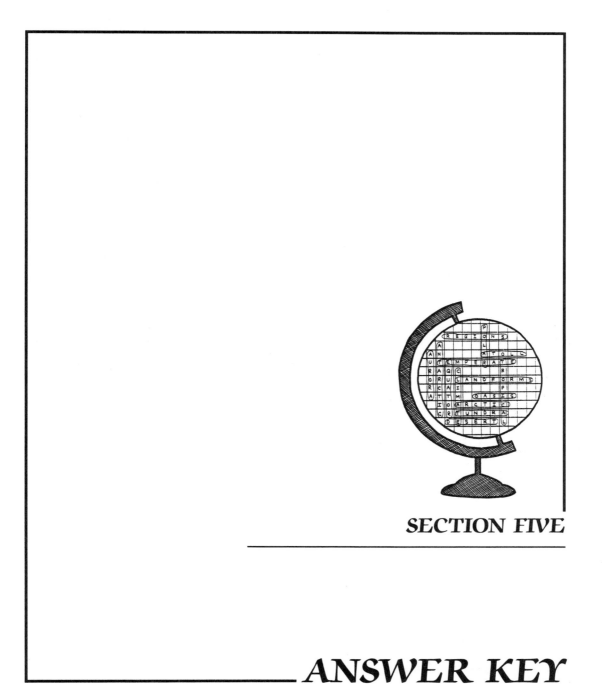

SECTION FIVE

ANSWER KEY

TRIBES WORD SEARCH

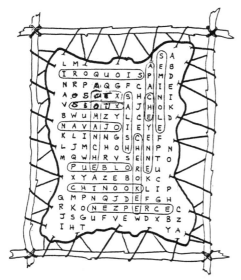

INDIANS AND PILGRIMS

1. met
2. sharing
3. might
4. many
5. shortage
6. skills
7. and
8. could
9. trees
10. feast

ANIMAL SKIN CLOTHING

Ready:
1. embers
2. embroider
3. tanned
4. velvet
5. fringed
6. repeated

Go:
1. fawn
2. false - (women)
3. tanned deer hide
4. moths - mothballs
5. men
6. bone needles,
   moose hair thread

WOODLAND CANOES

1. bark
2. hold
3. know
4. grows
5. large
6. cut
7. in
8. inside
9. with
10. make

WIGWAMS & LONGHOUSES

Ready:
1. wigwam
2. platform
3. hearth
4. sapling
5. slab
6. compartment

Go:
1. wigwam &
   longhouse
2. inward
3. birch bark,
   cattail mats
4. no
5. center
6. longhouse
7. cone

SEQUOYA'S ALPHABET

1. Hello
2. Hello. How
   are you?
3. Fine. How are you?
4. Fine. Thank you.

"THE DISH" MATH GAME

1. circle groups
   of 20
2. 9
3. Little Beaver
4. Lone Wolf
5. 200
6. less than

Bonus:
Falling Star and Little Beaver

PLAINS INDIANS CROSSWORD

1. tepee
2. parfleches
3. buffalo
4. tribes
5. nomads
6. buckskin
7. pemmican
8. plans
9. travois
10. tomahawk
11. antelope
12. moccasins

PLAINS INDIAN TIPIS

1. lived
2. homes
3. earth
4. together
5. stretched
6. joined
7. outside
8. have
9. down
10. set

ALL ABOUT THE BUFFALO

Ready:
1. moccasins
2. roamed
3. surround
4. pemmican
5. herds
6. utensils

Go:
1. buffalo
2. bows & arrows,
   stampeding
3. pemmican
4. yes
5. beef jerky
6. (answers will vary)
   they were all killed

THE TRAVOIS

1. today	6. along
2. move	7. carry
3. built	8. carry
4. apart	9. travois
5. make	10. twice

SACAJAWEA

1. born	6. on
2. child	7. trails
3. later	8. understand
4. study	9. carrying
5. Pacific	10. reach

HOGANS & PUEBLOS

Vocabulary - Ready:

1. sagebrush	4. canyon
2. adobe	5. remains
3. climate	6. dwelling

Comprehension - Go:

1. pueblos and hogans	4. ladders
2. straw, earth and clay	5. 200
3. pueblo	6. yes

KACHINAS

1. lived	6. gifts
2. learn	7. remind
3. kinds	8. wear
4. believed	9. end
5. decorated	10. good

AMAZING MAIZE MAZE

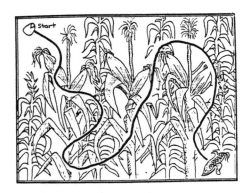

KIVAS

1. shape	6. performed
2. ground	7. of
3. brought	8. fires
4. important	9. see
5. kivas	10. not

SANDPAINTING MATH

1. 16 gallons	3. 56 quarts
2. 64 quarts	4. 1 quart

"KLAHOWYA SIKHS"

1. longhouse	8. spawn
2. costal	9. potlatch
3. salmon	10. canoe
4. ceremony	11. totem
5. basket	12. symbol
6. blanket	13. tribe
7. honor	

ALL ABOUT THE FIRST FISH

1. special, cycle, ceremony	4. edible
2. salmon	5. area
3. spawn	6. honor

1. salmon	4. fresh
2. Pacific	5. fish
3. yes	6. ceremony

LONGHOUSES

1. fresh	6. smoke
2. homes	7. used
3. shed	8. bark
4. were	9. thrown
5. no	10. covered

CANOES

1. transportation	6. into
2. canoes	7. stretch
3. rough	8. out
4. slowly	9. smooth
5. filled	10. finished

INDIAN STATE NAMES

1. Kansas	5. Illinois
2. Missouri	6. Iowa
3. Utah	7. Michigan
4. Arkansas	8. Alabama

INDIANS QUICK CHECK

1. Coastal	9. no
2. Plains	10. yes
3. Desert	11. yes
4. Woodland	12. no
5. Desert	13. yes
6. Coastal	14. yes
7. Plains	15. no
8. Woodland	

EXPLORERS WORD SEARCH

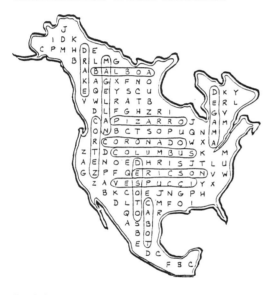

DISCOVERY MAZE

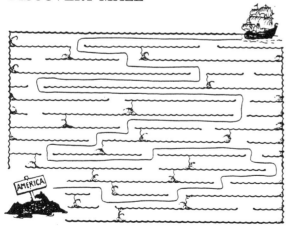

ALL ABOUT EARLY EXPLORERS

Ready:

1. circumnavigate	4. trade
2. route	5. spices
3. voyage	6. merchant

Go:

1. east	4. North America
2. an all water route	5. Pacific
3. west	6. circumnavigate

COLUMBUS WAS NOT FIRST

1. loved	6. sailed
2. explorers	7. map
3. almost	8. drawn
4. blown	9. before
5. North	10. visit

ALL ABOUT THE AZTECS

Ready:

1. warriors	4. calendars
2. water, ways	5. vanished
3. harvested	

Go:

1. Tenochtitlan	5. yes
2. chinampas	6. the god of growth
3. no	7. Spanish
4. glyphs	

THE LOST COLONY

1. they	6. believe
2. return	7. members
3. left	8. spoke
4. tree	9. been
5. lying	10. will

ALL ABOUT THE FIRST COLONIES

Ready:

1. survivors
2. valuable
3. established, founded
4. permanent
5. struggle
6. severe

Go:

1. English
2. yes
3. New Amsterdam
4. Indians
5. tobacco
6. Swedes
7. beaver

COLONIAL SCHOOLS

1. today
2. read
3. different
4. school
5. Lessons
6. paper
7. together
8. ink
9. children
10. taught

LINSEY–WOOLSEY

Wool: 4 - 5 - 1 - 3 - 2

Flax: 2 - 4 - 1 - 5 -3

ALL ABOUT THE BOSTON TEA PARTY

Ready:

1. cargo
2. protest
3. merchants
4. disguise
5. remove, repeal
6. required

Go:

1. King George III
2. Stamp Act
3. unfair
4. yes
5. no
6. 50
7. vote

HASTY PUDDING

1. 3
2. 6
3. 1
4. 4

5. 2
6. 5

*The corn was "more precious than silver."

REVOLUTION

Stamp Act–1765
Boston Tea Party–1773
Paul Revere's Ride–1775
Declaration of Independence– 1776
Articles of Confederation– 1777
British Recognize U.S. Independence– 1782
U.S. Constitution–1787
George Washington Elected President– 1789

ALL ABOUT THE CONSTITUTION

Ready:

1. democracy
2. decade
3. flexible
4. signature
5. framework
6. convention

Go:

1. 1787
2. 55
3. yes
4. Delaware
5. amendments
6. wasn't
7. 200

BILL OF RIGHTS

1. whether
2. Constitution
3. was
4. wrote
5. to
6. people
7. United
8. amendments
9. and
10. rights

WASHINGTON, D.C.

1. Pennsylvania Ave.
2. Washington Monument
3. Constitution Ave.
4. The Pentagon

GEORGE WASHINGTON

George Washington died in 1799
He was 68 when he died.

CITIZENSHIP WORD SEARCH

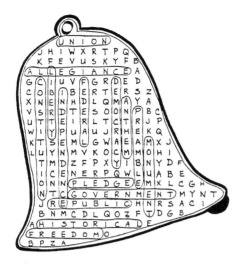

OUR NATIONAL ANTHEM

1. Few
2. until
3. written
4. near
5. battle
6. soldiers
7. began
8. from
9. above
10. tell

ALL ABOUT THE STATUE OF LIBERTY

Ready:

1. pedestal
2. frame
3. torch
4. teem
5. monument
6. shackle

Go:

1. France
2. 1884
3. yes
4. copper
5. spiral
6. no
7. shackle

ALL ABOUT THE PLEDGE OF ALLEGIANCE

Ready:

1. recite
2. solemn
3. pledge
4. indivisible
5. final
6. devotion

Go:

1. representative
2. 50
3. loyalty and devotion
4. no
5. yes
6. indivisible
7. justice

IMPORTANT EVENTS

1814 - 1884 - 1607
1775 - 1620 - 1787
1892 - 1789 - 1492

CITIZENSHIP CROSSWORD

1. liberty
2. monument
3. democracy
4. preamble
5. pledge
6. federal
7. anthem
8. freedom
9. allegiance
10. union
11. constitution
12. government

GOVERNMENT WORD SEARCH

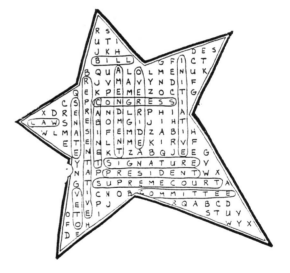

THREE BRANCHES

1. Representatives are elected by free vote
2. Someone who is elected to represent you
3. The plan for our government
4. Supreme Court - Judicial Branch - Settles Questions
5. Congress - Legislative Branch - Makes the Laws

6. The President - Executive Branch - Carries out the Laws
7. 2
8. answers will vary

CONGRESS

1. yes
2. no
3. no
4. no
5. yes
6. yes
7. yes

ALL ABOUT THE PRESIDENTS

Ready:

1. powerful
2. nation
3. tailor
4. executive
5. limited
6. famous

Go:

1. President
2. 4
3. Our President serves for limited time
4. no
5. Theodore Roosevelt
6. William Harrison
7. 40

THE SUPREME COURT

1. Court
2. if
3. justice
4. person
5. Supreme
6. their
7. make
8. decide
9. and
10. country

U.S. COINS

1. 63¢
2. 66¢
3. 32¢
4. 90¢
5. 36¢

VOTING!

1. Greeks
2. other
3. States
4. ballot
5. study
6. election
7. polling
8. ballot
9. instead
10. vote

A PRESIDENTIAL ELECTION

1. Candidate Declares
2. Primary Elections
3. Party Conventions
4. General Election
5. Electoral College
6. Inauguration Day

ALL ABOUT POLITICAL PARTIES

Ready:

1. major
2. minor
3. delegation, democracy
4. candidate
5. convention
6. nominate

Go:

1. delegate
2. Republican, Democratic
3. Abraham Lincoln
4. no
5. 4
6. democracy
7. a donkey

THE ELECTION'S END

1. election
2. ballot
3. campaign
4. precinct
5. candidate
6. convention
7. nominate
8. primary
9. delegates
10. registration
Bonus:
Inauguration

HERITAGE QUICK CHECK

1. Columbus
2. Asia
3. hardships
4. Hornbooks
5. lindsey-woolsey
6. tinderbox
7. hasty pudding
8. yes
9. no
10. yes
11. yes
12. yes
13. yes
14. no
15. no

CRISS-CROSS THE GLOBE

1. lines
2. two
3. of
4. globe

5. latitude   8. north
6. is   9. longitude
7. Canada   10. and

LATITUDE MATH

1. 23,23,46   3. 67°
2. 113°   4. 48°

Bonus: answers vary

GEOGRAPHY-REGIONS WORD SEARCH

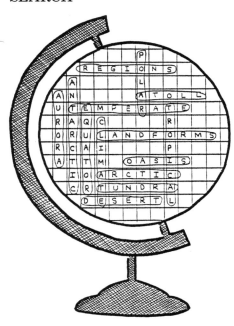

REGIONS OF THE WORLD CROSSWORD

Across: Down:

5. hemisphere   1. desert
7. tundra   2. temperate
10. temperature   3. latitude
12. atoll   4. north
14. coral   6. Equator
15. Arctic   8. permafrost
16. oasis   9. volcano
17. climate   11. resource
                13. Tropic

EQUINOX AND SOLSTICE

Northern Hemisphere	*Southern Hemisphere*
June 21st	December 21st
December 21st	June 21st
March 21st	September 22nd
September 22nd	March 21st

SEASONS

March 21st	September 22nd
June 21st	December 21st

ALL ABOUT THE ARCTIC REGIONS

Ready:

1. voles   4. tundra
2. thaws   5. permafrost
3. sponge   6. lichens

Go:

1. North Pole   5. yes
2. 3   6. Eskimos
3. tundra
4. voles and lemmings

HOW COLD IS IT?

1. −19° in March   5. It is winter in both regions.
2. −97° in August
3. Jan., Feb., March   6. Arctic Region
                    7. Antarctic Region
4. Nov., Dec., Jan.

Bonus: 7°-8° Arctic, −68 Antarctic

ESKIMOS

1. word   6. search
2. old   7. igloos
3. you   8. materials
4. several   9. and
5. lived   10. shared

ARCTIC HOMES

Ready:

1. igloo
2. sod
3. chink
4. snowhouse
5. temporary
6. semisub-
   terranean
7. blubber

Go:

1. igloo
2. tunnel
3. yes
4. whalebone
5. semisub-
   terranean
6. trees

ALL ABOUT THE ANTARCTIC REGION

Ready:

1. icecap
2. permanent
3. continents
4. average
5. interior
6. research

Go:

1. Antarctica
2. Atlantic, Pacific, Indian
3. 4-6 inches
4. blue whale
5. yes
6. fossils and petrified wood

WHAT IS AN AURORA?

1. poles
2. during
3. night
4. falling
5. are
6. off
7. space
8. atmosphere
9. light
10. southern

ALL ABOUT THE TROPICAL REGION

Ready:

1. atoll
2. evergreen
3. degree
4. coral
5. temperature
6. driest

Go:

1. Equator
2. Oceania or water hemisphere
3. animal
4. 100-150 inches
5. yes
6. rain forests

WHAT IS AN ATOLL?

1. inch
2. food
3. water
4. coral
5. left
6. years
7. above
8. sunken
9. ring
10. atoll

COCONUTS

1. tree
2. coconut
3. called
4. shell
5. white
6. meat
7. drink
8. bar
9. husk
10. woven

HAWAII & PUERTO RICO
Hawaii - A,E,F,H,I,J,L,N,O
Puerto Rico - B,C,D,G,H,J,K,M,N

ALL ABOUT THE SAHARA DESERT

Ready:

1. channel
2. oasis
3. underground
4. yearly
5. nomad
6. adapted

Go:

1. tropical
2. Africa
3. oasis
4. no
5. cactus
6. oil
7. 100°

ALL ABOUT THE TEMPERATE REGION

Ready:

1. determined
2. direct
3. population
4. season
5. hemisphere
6. climate

Go:

1. latitude
2. tropical
3. yes
4. temperate regions
5. true
6. North Temperate Region
7. January; answers may vary

ANIMALS OF THE TEMPERATE REGION

North:

3. bear, 4. beaver, 5. skunk

South:

1. kangaroo, 2. gorilla, 5. elephant

REGIONS' STORY PROBLEMS

1. 180 gallons of water
2. 73° colder
3. 2,989 square miles
4. 14,777 ft. You are working with numbers below zero (negative numbers) so you must add.

ALL ABOUT POPULATION

Ready:

1. billion
2. permanent
3. temperate
4. density
5. transportation
6. climate

Go:

1. population
2. 5
3. no
4. temperate
5. reason
6. Antarctica
7. high

GEOGRAPHY QUICK CHECK

1. seven
2. hemispheres
3. latitude
4. longitude
5. regions
6. tropical
7. temperate
8. yes
9. No
10. No
11. Yes
12. No
13. Yes
14. Yes